Trout
Biology

*An
Angler's
Guide*

Trout Biology

An Angler's Guide

W. B. WILLERS

THE UNIVERSITY OF WISCONSIN PRESS

Published 1981

The University of Wisconsin Press
114 North Murray Street
Madison, Wisconsin 53715

The University of Wisconsin Press, Ltd.
1 Gower Street
London WC1E 6HA, England

First printing

Printed in the United States of America

For LC CIP information see the colophon

ISBN 0-299-08720-4

For Karl Robert Willers

Contents

Illustrations

Color photos are found on pages 33-40.

Tables

Acknowledgments

I would like to express my gratitude to Robert Behnke of Colorado State University, W. Harry Everhart of Cornell University, and Vernon Hacker and Robert Hunt of the Wisconsin Department of Natural Resources for reading and criticizing parts of the manuscript. For the same reason thanks are due a number of my colleagues at the University of Wisconsin-Oshkosh: Todd Fonstad, Gerald Goldberger, James McKee, Nils Meland, William Sloey, Frederic Spangler, and David Wright. It was through David Wright's mathematical ability that the hypothetical trout population received suitable treatment.

Preface

Fisheries biologists have known for years that many trout anglers become so deeply engaged in trying to understand their prey that they read technical literature and write to researchers for reprints of articles appearing in biological journals. It's a rather surprising situation because such articles are intended to be read by specialists, and many require a background in biology to be understood without difficulty. Interest in trout biology, it seems, exists in abundance within the angling community.

The purpose of this book is to present some of the fundamentals of biology as they apply to salmonids and the relationship of these fish to their environment. It was written for people who like trout and with the primary intent to inform rather than entertain. Much of the information involves aspects of salmonid biology not frequently dealt with in angling literature, yet of more or less immediate concern to anglers. At the same time, I deal with such topics as food items and life cycles only in general terms, since these vary so much from one locale to another. An angler is really obliged to learn about the unique aspects of his home waters, and game and fish departments are always willing to supply information about in-state populations.

The book begins with a coverage of the evolution of salmonids in North America, then turns to the problems of trout breeding and hybridization. This is followed by a chapter on the structure and function of the salmonid body in which each of the body's systems is dealt with separately and in an order appropriate for a dissection in the field. Chapter 4 embraces the major groups of large parasites that have been able to invade the salmonid body and establish residence there.

The treatment of the aquatic medium in Chapter 5 is a prelude to the following two chapters, both of which deal with salmonid behavior. Chapter 6 is about nonreproductive behavior patterns, while Chapter 7 covers reproductive behavior and serves as a generalized view of the life cycle. Chapter 7 terminates with fertilization and subsequent hatching of eggs, and in so doing leads into the final chapter.

Chapter 8 differs from the other chapters in its very approach. A hypothetical population is created, and its changes through time are tabulated. Such use of models though standard practice among biologists, is not usually seen outside of technical literature. From what can be learned from the idealized population some appropriate steps for management are suggested.

Trout, salmon, and char collectively are called salmonids, since they are the best known (though not the only) fish in the Family Salmonidae. Quite often, however, I refer to salmonids in general as "trout," thereby using the latter in the rather loose way that anglers often do (as in "trout fly" and "trout rod"). I do so without apology, and only when the broad connotation is obvious.

With the exception of the brown trout, I've restricted coverage to species native to North America. The brown, since its introduction, has been of such great significance to angling on this continent that its omission would be a mistake.

Within biological literature there is a wealth of material pertinent to the interests of trout anglers. Anyone interested in getting copies of articles from technical journals would probably want to enlist the aid of a local librarian. For a nominal charge per page, copy-machine prints can usually be obtained through state libraries, which typically have close ties with state university systems where major biological journals are found.

Trout
Biology

*An
Angler's
Guide*

1.

Evolution in Salmonidae

And you are to note, that there are several kinds of Trouts: but these several kinds are not considered but by very few men; for they go under the general name of Trouts; just as pidgeons do, in most places; though it is certain, there are tame and wild pidgeons. . . .—IZAAC WALTON, 1676

Salmonid Origins

Trout and their close relatives are among the most primitive of fishes possessing bony skeletons, and a number of their physical traits link them to a major lineage that can be traced back some 100 million years. But "primitive" in this case doesn't mean structurally simple: biologically speaking, primitive characteristics — and primitive creatures — can be defined as those that have remained relatively unchanged over evolutionary time and that still resemble their ancestral forms.

The lineage itself, Salmoniformes, is incredibly diverse. In addition to salmonids, there are hosts of marine forms, most of them small, deep-sea creatures, some with bizarre shapes, huge jaws, and oversized, fanglike teeth. The only freshwater gamefish within the assemblage, aside from salmonids, is a group including the pickerel, northern pike, and muskellunge. The traits linking the trout group with this ancient lineage — skeletal features, patterns of dentition, and the like — are the sorts of things that would not be revealed by a superficial examination. But exactly where salmonids, as we know them, emerged from the vast array of forms has never been learned. The fossil record is simply too scanty.

The home of the salmonids is the Holarctic realm, which includes the northern latitudes of North America and Eurasia. For the most part, the waters containing these fish (the native range rather than waters into which they have been introduced by man) have become inhabited within the last 40,000 years. In geological terms this is a modest span of time, but in terms of changes that can be wrought within populations such a period may be significant, especially when creatures are introduced into new habitats.

3

Salmonids familiar to North American anglers have been heavily influenced by the geological activity of the Pleistocene epoch, which began perhaps 5 to 10 million years ago according to present estimates. During the Pleistocene there were four major episodes of continental glaciation separated by interglacial periods which often raised mean temperatures higher than those now experienced. At the height of each major advance vast sheets of ice covered the bulk of northern North America, rearranging the landscape and in the process modifying the ranges of salmonids.

The most recent of the four Pleistocene glaciations, known in North America as the Wisconsin episode, occurred within the last 40,000 years and was responsible for many of the geological features now visible. Perhaps 20,000 years ago the major advance slowed as temperatures in northern latitudes began to rise, and when the melting of the ice sheet exceeded the flow of ice from the north, retreat began. The process of deglaciation, which lasted for over 10,000 years and which involved the melting of millions of cubic miles of ice, gave rise to meltwater channels and to large lakes along the margins of the ice. Radiocarbon dating indicates that significant portions of the ice sheet remained in the upper Great Lakes region as recently as 10,000 years ago. The face of the land, already shaped by the scouring action of ice laden with rock, was further modified by the erosive action of pro-digious amounts of glacial melt with its load of suspended materials.

Not only was the distribution of existing salmonid species altered by all of this activity, but also in many areas physical barriers were established between populations of the same species. The separated populations, now unable to interbreed, evolved according to the specific demands of their particular new environments.

The Species Concept

To date, nearly a million and a half animal species have been recognized worldwide by biologists. In order to deal with these multitudes biologists have constructed an elaborate classification system that seeks to distinguish evolutionary relationships. This system of classes, orders, families, and a host of other categories is so huge and complex that anyone wanting to develop expertise has to limit himself to a certain chosen area of study within the Animal Kingdom. He must specialize.

The basic unit of the classification system is the species. Yet it is virtually impossible to define the concept of species in terms that will *always* hold true. Looking at a brown trout and a rainbow, one might sense through intuition that they are separate species; but when searching for criteria upon which to base a precise definition of species not many reliable criteria are found. Among biologists frequent disagreements arise regarding what do and do not constitute valid species, and salmonids offer some of the thorniest classification problems to be found.

Environmental influences in a particular locale can cause variations in color, general body shape, and a host of other physical features, making more difficult the task of figuring out what constitutes a valid species. Frequently trout have been formally (and mistakenly) described as species simply because a given population was darker or lighter or slimmer or heavier than other members of its species inhabiting different waters. The majority of these problems have now probably been worked out by biologists, but a lot of the old, erroneous scientific names are still seen sometimes in angling literature.

In general, a species is a group of individuals that resemble one another and are potentially capable of interbreeding, regardless of how geographically dispersed they might be. As a rule, members of one species don't breed with members of another, but this rule isn't iron-clad, since some different trout species (for instance) interbreed quite readily.

The scientific name of a species — such as *Salmo trutta,* the brown trout — is composed of two words, with the generic name (genus) given first, followed by the specific name. A genus might have a number of species within it: *Salmo trutta,* the brown trout, and *Salmo salar,* the Atlantic salmon, belong to the same genus and, it may be inferred, are more closely related to one another than either is to the brook trout, *Salvelinus fontinalis.*

Salmonids of North America

The Genus *Salmo*
Species of *Salmo,* generally considered to be the true trout, differ from other salmonids in that the shaft of the vomer, a bone in the roof of the mouth, is equipped with an alternating series (a zigzag row) of well-developed teeth. These fish possess dark spots on a light background, and 12 or fewer anal fin rays.

The various forms of *Salmo* have posed a major classification problem for biologists. Throughout the years at least 44 "species" have been described for the genus. More recently, however, greater stress has been placed on the concept that populations of a single species may vary considerably in superficial appearance. The general opinion at present seems to be that in western North America *most* populations of *Salmo* have evolved along one or the other of two major lines of descent — lines that are represented, generally, by the names "rainbow trout" and "cutthroat trout." In addition, there are a few indigenous groups apparently not closely related to either line: the Gila, Apache and red-banded trout, and the California golden, Mexican golden and Kern River golden trout.

The Rainbow Trout (Salmo gairdneri). Rainbows, in their typical coloration, have backs of blue to olive green, which fades to a silvery tone below. Along the lateral line there is a pink band, and back, sides, head, and fins are generally covered with a profusion of small black spots. As a rule, rainbow trout darken somewhat with age, and the pink lateral band deepens in color. But color variations are seen, many apparently due to local environmental conditions. Rainbows living in very clear lakes, for example, tend to be much lighter than those in more turbid waters, and sometimes lack the pink lateral band and the spots. A classic example of the effects of environment on outward appearance may be seen in the royal silver trout of Lake Tahoe, named *Salmo regalis* in 1912. Both rainbows and rainbow-cutthroat hybrids had been previously introduced into the lake. It has since been demonstrated that *Salmo regalis* is probably not a valid species, inasmuch as fish looking like royal silver trout can be produced simply by taking hatchery rainbows and raising them in Lake Tahoe.

The number of lateral line scales in rainbows ranges from 120 to 150; in the anal fin there are 10 to 12 rays. Although spring spawners by nature, fall-spawning strains have been developed.

The native range of the rainbow trout includes drainages of the Pacific coast from Alaska to Mexico and the waters of the Pacific Ocean. With the possible exception of several small areas, rainbows are not native east of the continental divide.

In much of their coastal range, rainbows cohabit with cutthroats. The ability to cohabit is considered a major criterion for species status; a true species, in other words, should be able to share an area with another species without interbreeding. Herein lies a problem. Where rainbows have been introduced into inland waters containing native populations of cutthroats, hybridization nearly always occurs. Nevertheless, the view that they constitute separate and valid species is virtually universal among biologists.

Fish that are normally resident in salt water, but which run to fresh water to spawn, are said to be "anadromous." Anadromous rainbows, as most anglers know, are called steelheads (though the term is also applied to large rainbows of the Great Lakes). In some coastal river systems cohabiting populations of steelheads don't interbreed simply because they have different spawning times — "winter runs" and "summer runs" — a phenomenon giving rise to "seasonal" races, or strains. Seasonal races may cohabit with resident stocks of nonanadromous rainbows; all belong to the same species, but because their uses of the environment are different, members of the different populations do not interbreed, and the integrity of each population is maintained. If the reproductive isolation of cohabiting populations is absolute, each will evolve as independently as they might if separated by a mountain range. (The original causes of reproductive isolation are not known. A prevalent theory holds that irregularities during the last glacial retreat, in which minor advances of ice could have split populations temporarily, created opportunities for variations in spawning habits to evolve. With the final retreat of the glacial barrier the populations may have been reunited, but their differing life histories prevented interbreeding and they evolved separately.)

If two or more forms within a species exhibit consistent differences — and if those differences aren't a result of merely local environmental influences — biologists may classify them as subspecies. There are no consistent anatomical differences between anadromous steelheads and nonanadromous rainbows that would justify subspecific designations. In fact, anadromous stocks have been used to establish nonanadromous populations in new waters. But nonanadromous rainbows are still occasionally referred to as *Salmo gairdneri irideus* (indicating them as a subspecies of *Salmo gairdneri*); names, once established in the literature, are slow to die.

Rainbow trout were first introduced by man into waters outside their native range in 1874. By 1880 stockings had been made in a number of eastern and midwestern states, and by 1971 they had become established in 39 states in which they were not originally native. There have been no reports of anadromous steelhead runs in East Coast states. Rainbows are now found in all of the provinces of Canada except the Northwest Territories, and on all continents but Antarctica.

The Cutthroat Trout (Salmo clarki). The native distribution of cut-throat trout is in coastal streams from Alaska's Prince William Sound to California's Eel River and, within the interior of North America, in the Great Basin and the drainages of the South Saskatchewan and upper Colorado rivers, as well as the Colorado drainages of the Platte and Arkansas rivers. Although some coastal populations are sea-run, they tend to stay closer to estuaries than do the more completely anadromous steelheads. Seasonal races don't occur, nor do cohabiting populations of anadromous and nonanadromous cutthroats.

As might be expected in a species with a broad geographical range, there are some variations in spawning times. Along the coast cut-throats tend to breed in February and March; interior populations spawning later, often in April or May.

Cutthroats are named for their most obvious identifying feature, the red slash marks just below the gill covers and lower jaws. Their lateral line scale count is more than 150. But the general color and ex-ternal markings of the species vary widely from one population to another throughout its range. As a result, a number of populations were incorrectly described as bona fide, distinct species during an era in which the diversity possible within a single species wasn't fully ap-preciated. Cutthroat classification has a slight air of confusion about it.

Among the various forms of cutthroats two are especially prevalent, and may be distinguished by characteristics of their spotting. Frequently referred to as "coastal cutthroats" *(Salmo clarki clarki)* and "interior cutthroats" *(Salmo clarki lewisi)*, these fish are commonly given the status of subspecies (Figure 1.1, color photo, p. 33). Although the former is characterized by a profusion of small spots, while the lat-ter has fewer but larger spots, there are no consistent differences in their gross physical features that would allow for a legitimate separa-tion of the two. On the other hand, biologists using chromosome counts to help determine relationships among cutthroat populations have found that each cell of the coastal form has 70 chromosomes, while the count for the interior form is 64. Chromosomes are visible structures present in nearly all cells of the body, and the number per cell is usual-ly fixed for all members of a species. Naturally, this finding in cut-throats reinforces the view that the two fish are distinct from one another, and could be used as a potent argument by anyone of the opinion that they should be regarded as separate species.

Comparisons of chromosomes have been used to help determine the relationship of the highly distinctive Snake River cutthroat to other cutthroats. This fish (Figure 1.2, color photo, p. 34), found in the river below Jackson Lake, Wyoming, has the profusion of small spots characteristic of the coastal cutthroat, yet in surrounding areas the typical large-spotted interior cutthroat abounds. The Snake River variety is also unusual in that, in its native habitat, it has hybridized neither with rainbows nor with other strains of cutthroat trout. While these traits suggest that it might be a geographically isolated representative of the coastal cutthroat, its chromosome count is identical to those for interior cutthroats. There are biologists now who feel that the Snake River trout should be considered a subspecies, though formal description has not occurred at the time of this writing. (A "formal" description requires a carefully written report of anatomic features, naming according to an elaborate set of rules, and publication in an appropriate scientific journal.)

Among cutthroats of the interior, the Lahontan cutthroat trout *(Salmo clarki henshawi)* and the Colorado greenback trout *(Salmo clarki stomias)* are considered by many to be valid subspecies because they do possess distinctive and consistent characters — more gill rakers in the former, more scales in the latter, different spotting in each (Figures 1.3, color photo, p. 34, 1.4, and 1.5, color photo, p. 35).

Figure 1.4. A rare photo of the original Lahontan cutthroat trout. The fish were caught in the Truckee River about 1918. (Courtesy of S. S. Wheeler and Caxton Press, Caldwell, Idaho.)

A major problem in stocking cutthroats has been the ease with which they hybridize with rainbows introduced into waters formerly the province of cutthroats alone. The result has been a wide-scale dilution of many cutthroat strains. It is surprising that in coastal areas, where cutthroat trout cohabit with anadromous steelheads (though rarely with nonanadromous rainbows), interbreeding does not occur, while in inland areas hybridization nearly always occurs — with fertile offspring as a result. The hybridization problem has been compounded by past practices in the propagation of hatchery trout. Eggs from a variety of sources were used without any particular care being taken to maintain the purity of cutthroat strains.

The spin-off of all this interbreeding has been that the cutthroat trout of many areas represent mixtures of strains, most commonly through the addition of some rainbow blood. Just within the last century perhaps 99 percent of the unique cutthroat strains of interior drainages have been lost forever. The species has fared badly at our hands, its tremendous diversity having been drastically reduced.

A case in point is the huge Lahontan cutthroat *(Salmo clarki henshawi)* that was once found in the waters of Pyramid Lake, Nevada. This subspecies may well have been the largest representative of *Salmo* in North America, with weights up to 60 pounds having been reported. During the last spawning run, which took place in 1938 (access to spawning areas thereafter was blocked by dams), a collection was made of 195 specimens that averaged 20 pounds. What today is referred to as *Salmo clarki henshawi* is, in fact, of a different lineage and has an infusion of rainbow trout blood. In Pyramid Lake, the maximum weights now attained by Lahontans are roughly a third of those attained by the original native population.

Many formally described subspecies of interior cutthroats are now extinct, and most of those remaining are extremely rare. But there still exist some strains, whose distribution is limited, that may ultimately be described as subspecies.

Other Forms of Salmo in Western North America. Some western populations of *Salmo* appear to be fairly independent of both cutthroat and rainbow lineages. For the most part they have been considered as distinct species, even though they commonly interbreed with other forms of *Salmo.* Hybridization resulting from indiscriminate stocking has brought some dangerously close to extinction. Perhaps the best known of these groups are the spectacularly colored golden trout of the Sierra Nevada.

In 1972 Pierre Legendre and his colleagues published the results of a comparison of forms of *Salmo* of uncertain lineage:

California golden trout *(S. aguabonita aguabonita)* — native to parts of the Kern River drainage of California (Figure 1.6, color photo, p. 35)

Kern River trout *(S. aguabonita gilberti)* — also native to the Kern River

Gila Trout *(S. gilae)* — native to the Gila River, New Mexico (Figure 1.7, color photo, p. 36).

Mexican golden trout *(S. chrysogaster)* — found in three rivers along Mexico's Pacific coast

Apache trout *(S. apache)* — native to Arizona's Salt River

Rio Truchas trout (not formally described) — native to Rio Truchas, Mexico

"Red-banded trouts" (not formally described) — a group of related, but geographically disconnected populations found in Oregon and northern California (Figure 1.8, color photo, p. 36).

Specimens from each of these groups were compared to one another, to large-spotted interior cutthroats, and to rainbows. Data involving eight physical features, including coloration, spotting, and various morphometric and meristic[1] traits were analyzed by two different computer-aided techniques; these put the relationships of the fish into diagram form (Figures 1.9 and 1.10).

Diagrams like this should not be taken as gospel, however, because it's hard to say to what degree any one trait mirrors true relationships. A computer just handles the numbers fed into it, and people have to make judgements about the relative importance of the numbers. In this case, even though the two comparison techniques generally yielded similar results, the Mexican golden trout fell into different locations in each of the relationship diagrams.

The Brown Trout (Salmo trutta). Browns aren't native to our continent, of course, but their impact on trout fishing in America has been so enormous that their exclusion from this account would be a mistake. These fish tend toward a shade of brown on the back and sides — olive brown, golden brown, perhaps even with a hint of green. This fades

---

1. Morphometric comparisons deal with measurements (e.g., length, circumference), while meristic comparisons deal with counts of structures occurring in series. For fish, meristic counts are commonly made of scales, fin rays, gill rakers, vertebrae, pyloric ceca, and branchiostegal rays.

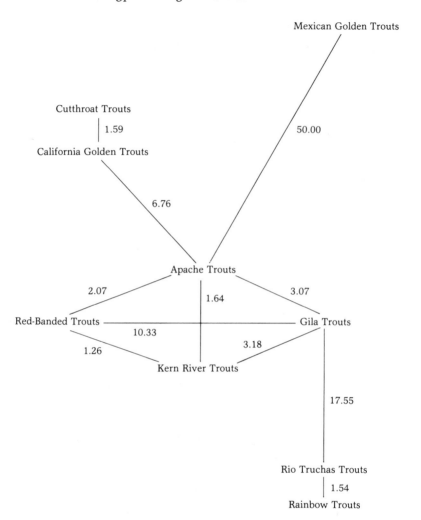

Figure 1.9. Relationships of some salmonids based on clustering analysis. (Redrawn from Legendre, *et al.*, 1972.)

into a yellow or cream-colored belly. Spots are generally large, and most are dark brown or black, although there is also a sprinkling of red or orange; the spots normally have a light halo around them. Browns have a lateral line scale count of from 115 to 150.

As in some other salmonids, brown trout specimens from clear lakes tend to be lighter in color, and this tendency is sometimes so pronounced that browns take on the silver tone of landlocked salmon. The two can be distinguished by checking the vomerine teeth: in landlocks, the two rows of teeth are close together and may even give the impression of being a single row; brown trout have two clearly separate rows.

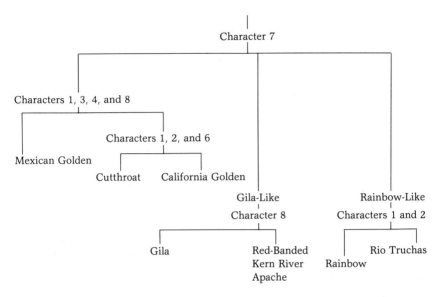

Figure 1.10. Relationships of some salmonids based on CHARANAL computer analysis. (Redrawn from Legendre, *et al.,* 1972.)

    The native waters of the brown trout occur throughout continental Europe, in the British Isles and Iceland, and in parts of western Asia and North Africa. These fish are generally considered to be fall spawners, but in some areas they are found breeding during the winter, sometimes as late as January or February.

    Like cutthroats, brown trout from different areas may exhibit many variations in external appearance. For this reason a host of scientific names has been incorrectly applied to them. In Europe, where these fish inhabit diverse waters, it has long been customary to use *Salmo trutta* for anadromous browns, *Salmo fario* for populations found in flowing waters, and *Salmo lacustris* for lake-inhabiting populations. This practice commits the sin of applying scientific names on the basis of habitat use rather than evolutionary relationship. But in any case biologists, on the basis of a substantial body of information, now favor the view that all of the various forms of brown trout belong to the single variable species, *Salmo trutta.*

    Browns were widely distributed during the Pleistocene epoch, but their preglacial ancestry hasn't been adequately determined. Like rainbows, they have had their range extended by introductions to all continents except Antarctica. They were introduced into the United States in 1883 when eggs of German origin were brought over to be hatched in Michigan. The "Loch Leven strain" was imported from the British Isles to Canada in 1884, and to the United States the following year. Brown trout are presently found in 34 states and nine Canadian provinces. They have proven less popular in Canada than in the United States and only Alberta and Nova Scotia still maintain stocking programs. Fish culture practices have tended toward the interbreeding of stocks, and for the most part, strain identification in North America is no longer practical, if indeed possible.

The Atlantic Salmon and the Landlocked Salmon (Salmo salar). A "salmon," by popular definition, is a salmonid that lives the bulk of its life at sea and runs to fresh water to spawn — at least that has been the more or less traditional use of the term. But the definition breaks down when one considers that some "salmon" are landlocked and can't reach the sea, and that some "trout," such as the steelhead, behave like salmon in being anadromous. So the uses of "salmon" and "trout" are really dictated largely by custom. And the Atlantic salmon, being a species of *Salmo*, is quite closely related to brown trout, rainbows, and other species of the genus.

During their life at sea, and when beginning a spawning run into fresh water, Atlantic salmon have a back of dark blue or brown. The rest of the body is silver, with small black spots typically in the form of an X. As a run progresses upstream the body darkens quite a bit, the female becoming black and the male a reddish color. Scales in the lateral line range from 106 to 125 in number.

Spawning runs take place in late summer and early autumn when the fish make their way up rivers and into shallow tributary streams, where the eggs are deposited. The eggs hatch in springtime, and the resulting young remain in fresh water until they grow to a length of five or six inches, a process which normally requires one to three years, but which may take as many as seven years. Now known as "smolts," they take on a silvery hue and migrate downstream to the sea where they feed, grow and mature before returning — commonly three to five years later — to their parent stream to spawn. A few individuals may make several migrations during their lives, but repeat spawners generally make up less than 10 percent of a given run. Some Atlantic salmon make a spawning migration after having spent only a single year in the ocean; these tend to weigh in the neighborhood of 4 pounds, rather than the 9 to 12 pounds typical of older fish. Anglers call these small specimens "grilse."

Whereas species such as cutthroats and browns have highly variable populations, the opposite is true of *Salmo salar*, which shows surprising uniformity throughout its native range. Sea-run Atlantic salmon from Europe and North America mingle freely on their common feeding grounds off the coast of Greenland, but because of their separate spawning areas, the two groups don't interbreed. And because each fish tends to spawn in the stream where it spent its early life, some isolation of breeding groups occurs even in neighboring river systems. A small percentage of fish do stray, however.

As it happens, the Atlantic salmon of North America and those of Europe possess differences in blood chemistry. Because this provides a measure of proof that interbreeding between the two hasn't taken place for a long period of time, a few biologists prefer to recognize them as two subspecies. But this approach hasn't been widely accepted.

There is general agreement that the nonanadromous populations called "ouananiche" and "landlocked salmon" which are found naturally in some fresh waters of North America are recent offshoots of sea-run ancestors. The former is native to some Canadian waters, while the latter is characteristically found farther south in the northeastern United States. Though they are often referred to as *Salmo salar ouananiche* and *Salmo salar sebego*, respectively, most biologists feel that there are not sufficient grounds for subspecific designations. But there are slight physical differences between the two, so it is reasonable to suppose that they arose separately from sea-run stocks.

The native waters of North American freshwater populations consist of lakes and drainages of low elevation that were recently contiguous with saltwater. It is the majority opinion among authorities that freshwater forms developed when anadromous populations lost their access to the ocean during postglacial fluctuations in sea levels. However, this "glacial barrier hypothesis" is not universally accepted. Those holding an opposing view note that freshwater populations now having access to the sea fail to use it, and that there are variations in life cycles among sea-run populations. In the northern extremity of the range, young fish (salmon "parr") often remain in fresh water for extended periods — sometimes as long as seven years — and some individuals reach sexual maturity before their migration to the sea. Extremely cold conditions characteristic of the northern parts of the range, and certainly found farther to the south during glacial epochs, may have retarded the migratory urge to a greater degree than sexual development; under such conditions, some fish may well have established freshwater populations. According to this hypothesis, the "landlocked" condition (in such cases) would have been a result of geological changes that took place *after* development of exclusively freshwater life cycles.

The Pacific Salmons (Genus *Oncorhynchus*)
Species of the Pacific salmon group come from the same general lineage that gave rise to the various forms of *Salmo* in western North America. But preglacial evolutionary patterns for salmonids aren't well understood, and there's disagreement as to when a split into two branches might have taken place. Nevertheless, even though *Salmo* and *Oncorhynchus* are much alike anatomically, there is evidence that they've been distinct lineages for a very long time. The fossil skull shown in Figure 1.11 came from a salmonid that lived during the Pliocene, an epoch that ended perhaps 5 to 10 million years ago. This fossil bears a stronger resemblance to *Oncorhynchus* than to *Salmo*.

Like *Salmo*, the spotting on Pacific salmon is dark on a lighter background. But *Oncorhynchus* has 13 to 19 anal fin rays, compared to 12 or fewer for *Salmo*, and the vomerine teeth of the Pacific salmon, in

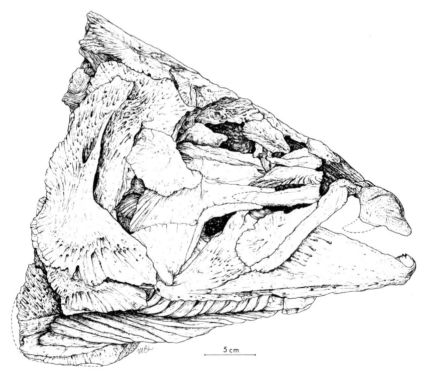

Figure 1.11. The skull of a fossil salmonid, *Smilodonichthyes rastrosus*. The skeletal structure is similar to that of *Oncorhynchus*, and if the relationship of skull to body length was the same as it is in present-day Pacific salmons, the length of this individual was a bit over six feet (the skull is 18 inches long). The species is believed to have existed about six or seven million years ago. (Printed by permission of Ted M. Cavender, Curator of Fishes, Museum of Zoology, Ohio State University.)

contrast to those of *Salmo,* are weakly developed and might even be lost in older fish.

The Pacific salmon is distributed in a broad arc across the North Pacific from California up to Alaska, across Siberia, and as far west as Formosa. The genus is represented in North America by five species which, for the time being at least, appear to have generated no major classification problems.

> Chinook, or king salmon *(Oncorhynchus tschawytscha)*
> Coho, or silver salmon *(Oncorhynchus kisutch)*
> Sockeye, or red salmon *(Oncorhynchus nerka)*
> Pink salmon *(Oncorhynchus gorbuscha)*
> Chum salmon *(Oncorhynchus keta)*

Spawning takes place, depending upon species and location, from June to February. Young fish may migrate downstream to salt water immediately after emerging from the stream bed, as pink salmon do, or they may remain in the parent stream for two or three years, as is the case with sockeyes. Time spent at sea ranges from two to eight years. All Pacific salmon die after their one and only spawning run.

The sockeye salmon *(Oncorhynchus nerka)* is represented not only by anadromous populations, but also by numerous nonanadromous populations usually called "kokanee." These little fish rarely exceed 20 inches in length. Since young anadromous sockeyes normally spend two or three years in fresh water before migrating to the sea, there is plenty of opportunity for the establishment of exclusively freshwater life cycles. So it's highly probable the various populations of kokanee evolved independently from anadromous stocks.

The Chars (Genus *Salvelinus)*

In their daily speech, North American anglers don't distinguish between trout and char, preferring to lump them all under the name of "trout" (the "Arctic char" is an exception). Even biologists have acquiesced to popular terminology, referring to "brook trout" and "lake trout" rather than "brook char" and "lake char." Strictly speaking, the popular usage is incorrect, but then there really aren't any rules pertaining to the use of common names.

Chars have a skull structure that sets them apart from other salmonids: the vomer, in the roof of the mouth, is rather boat-shaped and is lightly toothed. At a more practical level, chars can be distinguished by their light spots on a darker background, and by their scales, which are especially tiny. The chars' lateral line scale counts are above 190.

As in the case of *Salmo,* the genus *Salvelinus* in North America presents a number of unresolved problems. It does appear that an early split in the ancestral tree gave rise to the Arctic char-Dolly Varden lineage on the one hand, and the lake trout-brook trout lineage on the other. Subsequent splits yielded the species familiar to anglers today. This being so, brook trout and lake trout are more closely related to one another than either one is to the Arctic char or the Dolly Varden.

The Arctic Char (Salvelinus alpinus). The Arctic char is a species in which physical variations are so numerous that one sometimes sees references to the "*Salvelinus alpinus* complex." These fish are found across northern North America and Eurasia, and in Greenland and Iceland. In North America they occur both in anadromous and nonanadromous populations and, by and large, are characteristic of areas not too far removed from salt water.

Arctic char look like big brook trout, but lack the vermiculation — the wormlike pattern — characteristic of the upper part of the brook trout body. On their dorsal surfaces Arctic char may be shades of green, blue or brown; the sides are often a bright orange, but may be a light steely blue, perhaps with a trace of pink. Spots which are relatively sparse, range from cream to a bright red orange. The pectoral, pelvic, and anal fins are orange with a white leading edge, and a black stripe between the white and the orange.

Migration to the sea is an annual event in anadromous Arctic char populations. In springtime the fish move down to salt water, where they tend to remain close to river mouths. When they run back to fresh water to spawn and to overwinter, they have the silver hue so common to sea-run salmonids, but their bright coloration soon returns.

In eastern North America there are several isolated Arctic char populations in recently glaciated lakes: the blueback "trout" (*Salvelinus oquossa*) of Maine, the Sunapee "trout" (*Salvelinus aureolus*) of New Hampshire (Figure 1.12, color photo, p. 37), and Marsten's "trout" or the red "trout" (*Salvelinus marstoni*) of Quebec. Though these have been described as separate species, as the scientific names indicate, anatomic and chemical comparisons show no consistent differences from *Salvelinus alpinus;* it would therefore appear that their designations as separate species are not justified.

The Dolly Varden (Salvelinus malma). The Dolly Varden is a fall spawner with a native range extending from northern California to the Aleutians and from eastern Siberia to Japan and Korea. Both anadromous and nonmigratory populations exist. Though Dolly

Vardens are characteristically found in river systems feeding into the Pacific, naturally occurring populations may be found in some waters of the eastern slope of the Rockies. In southwest Alaska the range of the Dolly Varden overlaps with that of the closely related Arctic char, but hybridization rarely, if ever, takes place.

A current theory has it that the common ancestor of Arctic chars and Dolly Vardens probably was distributed continuously from the Atlantic to the Pacific, occupying essentially the ranges now held by the present species. Sometime during the Pleistocene geographical barriers developed that allowed the separate species to evolve.

Dolly Vardens look a lot like Arctic char, but unlike the latter their spots extend onto the back. Some Dolly Vardens also resemble brook trout, but their backs usually lack the vermiculations typical of brook trout, and even when vermiculations are evident they are relatively weakly defined.

The Dolly Varden presents a situation somewhat analogous to that of the interior cutthroat trout, since a number of Dolly Varden forms are found in North America. Notable among these are a form found north of the Alaska Peninsula and a form found south of that peninsula and in the Aleutian chain. There is also an interior form. Biologists generally agree that the different forms of Dolly Varden have resulted from isolation of the species into regional populations, and that much, if not most, of this isolation was caused by glacial activity. In each region there has been enough differentiation within the population to make its members fairly distinct from Dolly Vardens in other regions.

Some forms of the Dolly Varden probably represent valid subspecies, but few formal descriptions have been published. In 1973 a new species, *Salvelinus anakuvukensis,* was described from an isolated portion of Alaska's Brooks Range, but there isn't much doubt that the fish is a part of the Dolly Varden line.

The Lake Trout (Salvelinus namaycush). Until fairly recently lake trout were considered to constitute a separate genus, *Cristivomer,* and this generic name is still frequently seen in various writings. But new information has brought the species into *Salvelinus,* and almost everybody agrees that's the right place for it.

The native range of the lake trout is restricted to the North American continent from Alaska and British Columbia eastward to Labrador (although they don't occur in Newfoundland), and from the Arctic Ocean southward to New England, the Great Lakes, and the headwaters of the Mississippi and Missouri River drainages. Lake trout normally inhabit deep, cold lakes, but they can also be found in rivers entering or exiting such lakes.

Lake trout are less colorful than other salmonids. Their background colors are shades of gray or olive green, and their bodies are densely covered with pale spots. Even during the spawning season, at which time a salmonid's coloration is most vivid, there is little more in these fish than the development of a rosy hue on the fins.

Lake trout spawn in autumn or early winter by broadcasting their eggs onto rock or gravel lake bottoms in water up to 100 feet deep. This is rather unusual salmonid behavior, because most salmonids construct — or at least attempt to construct — depressions in which their eggs are deposited and covered with gravel. The eggs of lake trout are simply let loose onto hard bottom and left to roll about, perhaps to find some protection if chance carries them into cracks or depressions.

In marked contrast to highly variable species like the Arctic char, the lake trout exhibits a surprising degree of uniformity throughout its extensive range. The reasons for this remain speculative. One hypothesis is that lake trout, generally found in a specific habitat (deep water) rather than in diverse habitats, have avoided the broad spectrum of environmental pressures that would normally lead to the development of different subgroups. Another view is that the deepwater existence of lake trout has afforded them a shield from cosmic radiation, as a result of which they have a lower rate of mutation than species in shallower waters.

But even though lake trout are quite uniform in appearance, careful comparisons have indicated at least five major subdivisions of the species. Each may be identified according to its area of distribution: the Arctic, the Peace River system, the Pacific drainage, the Hudson Bay drainage, and the Atlantic drainage. Each probably arose from stocks surviving the last continental glaciation in their respective unglaciated refuge areas.

The waters of Lake Superior contain two cohabiting forms of lake trout — a typical "lean" trout and a deep-bodied trout known locally as the "siscowet" (Figure 1.13). In addition to differences in general body outline, there are consistent structural and chemical differences between the two. Furthermore, the siscowet usually inhabits deeper waters than do typical lake trout. Apparently interbreeding doesn't take place. The siscowet has been referred to as everything from a true species to merely a typical trout that has been modified by the local en-

Figure 1.13. The bottom fish represents a typical lake trout; the upper fish is a siscowet. Both were taken in Lake Superior. (Courtesy of Bruce Swanson, Wisconsin Department of Natural Resources.)

vironment. The present consensus is that it deserves subspecies recognition as *Salvelinus namaycush siscowet;* this being so, the typical form becomes *Salvelinus namaycush namaycush.*

The Brook Trout *(Salvelinus fontinalis).* Heavy vermiculations on the back are perhaps the most obvious identifying feature of the brook trout. Background coloration can be anywhere from a light silvery blue to a dark green. Among the lighter spots covering the body are red ones with halos of red, yellow, or off-white. As in some of the other chars, the lower fins are orange with white leading edges. Brook trout spawn in the fall.

The original native range of the brook trout extended along the coast of northeastern North America as far south as New York and New Jersey, and from this area westward as far as eastern Manitoba and the Great Lakes. To the north brookies were found in waters feeding into Hudson Bay, and to the south in a fingerlike range coinciding with the Appalachian Mountains as far as Georgia. Sea-run brook trout, sometimes called ''coasters'' or ''salters,'' have been observed in coastal portions of the range from Cape Cod to Hudson Bay.

Like rainbows and brown trout, brookies have had their range extended greatly by introduction into new waters. They are now familiar to anglers in western North America, and are also found in South America, Europe, Asia, Africa, and New Zealand.

Brook trout, unlike lakers, haven't become specialized for a particular habitat. They are found in a variety of waters from mere trickling streams to large northern lakes. Nevertheless, like lake trout, brook trout exhibit a high degree of uniformity throughout their range. There seems to be no suitable, widely held hypothesis to explain this high degree of evolutionary stability.

Clear-cut examples of cohabiting brook trout strains are rare, and only two such populations have been verified. The "silver char," which shared a New Hampshire lake with typical brook trout, was first described as a species (*Salvelinus agassizii*), and was thought by some to be of Arctic char lineage. The "aurora trout," found in an Ontario lake in cohabitation with typical brookies, was originally described as *Salvelinus timagamiensis* (Figure 1.14, color photo, p. 38). Both strains were linked with the book trout lineage through later studies.

The silver char hasn't been seen for decades, and is most certainly extinct; only 13 preserved specimens remain. It is probable that promiscuous stocking of outside strains broke down the reproductive barriers that once existed between silver char and the typical brookies native to their common waters. The distinctive characteristics of silver char were then lost through incorporation into the homogeneous population. The same process may have eliminated the aurora trout in Ontario. Though hybrids of aurora trout and typical brookies were reported in the 1960s, Dr. W. B. Scott, curator of the Royal Ontario Museum, stated in a letter to me dated May 10, 1974, "So far as I am aware, the aurora trout is no longer extant. It appears to have disappeared from its former range, and as far as I known living specimens do not exist."

There are few unequivocal answers to questions about evolutionary histories and relationships among salmonids, so classification has involved some differences of opinion. The relationship tree in Figure 1.15 is based on a tree published by Robert Behnke, and reflects his interpretation of the available data. I have modified his tree by omitting some salmonids not native to North America. The time scale, which wasn't part of the original figure, was correlated to the tree by Dr. Behnke at my request.

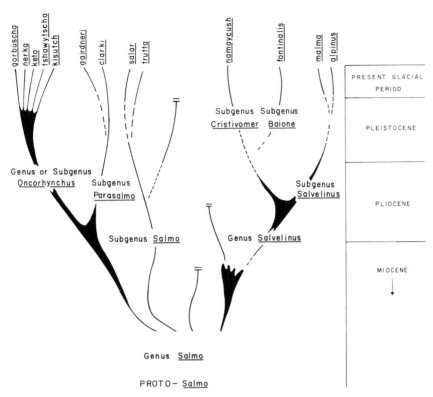

Figure 1.15. A suggested phylogeny of salmonids of North America. (Modified from Behnke, 1968, Mitt. Hamburg Zool. Mus. Inst. 66:1-15.) The figure has been redrawn to omit some groups native to areas outside of North America (seen as dead ends on the figure.)

2.

Inheritance in Trout

In such a plastic group as the Salmonidae there are all shades of differentiation from the species down almost to the individual.

—GEORGE A. ROUNSEFELL, 1962

Trout Breeding and Some of Its Problems

The breeding of salmonids presents a particular problem. Domesticated creatures obviously differ in some respects from their wild brethren, and in most cases this poses few problems if the domestic strains are destined to cope with nothing more than the relatively mild demands of the household or the barnyard. But hatchery-bred trout, in order to remain essentially creatures of the wild, should retain a good measure of the toughness of their forebears.

The basic hereditary mechanism is precisely the same for wild trout and for domestic strains raised in hatcheries. In both cases genes, which are contained in the chromosomes of the body cells, are the units that control the development of the multitudes of hereditary characters. And in both cases the selection of certain fish as breeders determines which genes will be passed on to subsequent generations. In the case of hatchery trout, the selection of parent fish is made by people on the basis of qualities thought to be desirable. In the wild, however, selection is determined objectively by an environment substantially harsher than that of a hatchery, where conditions are carefully controlled to allow maximum survival. A natural environment imposes a host of stressing conditions which must be faced by all members of a population, and the process of natural selection favors survival of and reproduction by those individuals best equipped for contending with the conditions. Breeders in wild populations are selected strictly on their demonstrated ability to survive and endure.

The genetic makeup of any population is aptly called the "gene pool." Prevalent genes within a gene pool (i.e., within a population) have persisted because the traits they give rise to have favored survival.

So it follows that a wild trout population existing over a long period of time within a relatively stable set of conditions is particularly well suited to its environment. Its gene pool may be substantially different than that of a nearby, but reproductively isolated, population of the same species.

The genes that determine obvious traits such as color are only a small portion of a trout's total genetic makeup. Of the many thousands of genetically determined traits, most are inevitably concealed from view. The myriad biochemical pathways ultimately responsible for growth patterns, the metabolism of foods, etc., may not create the intense visual "noise" of black spots on a rose-colored lateral line, but any one of them might be of far greater importance in determining survival ability.

Strains of trout produced under hatchery conditions probably harbor — to a greater extent than wild trout — genes that would be selected against by a natural environment. In any given generation of hatchery trout, survival will be much higher (barring epidemics) than would be the case in nature, because so many natural stresses have been substantially done away with. In the hatchery, abilities to compete for food or to avoid predators are not factors that dictate daily whether an individual is to remain on the scene. This simply means that trout which would perish in a more hostile environment can survive to maturity.

From such a generation of hatchery trout the parent stock for the generation to follow will be chosen. Man generally makes choices on the basis of a limited number of discernible characters that normally include size, general body shape and coloration, and since economics enters into the trout breeding picture, growth rate and egg yield also receive attention. Vitality and gameness may also be detectable and used as criteria in choosing brood stock. But inevitably, not all of the traits favoring survival will be detected. Genes are inherited independently of one another, so the fact that a given trout is big and bright says nothing about the many indiscernible genetic traits that have a bearing on the ability to survive.

As an example, the physical ability to endure prolonged or repeated stress from a variety of sources is not the sort of thing normally bred for, yet wild trout live in a stress-producing world. So it's not surprising that the survival rates of hatchery trout introduced into natural waters are typically lower than those of wild trout. This is illustrated by a study that compared a wild strain of brook trout with

brook trout of a strain that had been domesticated for many generations. Fish of both groups were raised under identical conditions. The
domestic trout grew faster, but they possessed less stamina than the
wild trout; moreover, the domestic brookies were less wary and tended
not to conceal themselves.

None of this means that the breeding and rearing of hatchery
trout are pursuits without justification. It simply points out pitfalls of
which biologists are very much aware, and it shows the basis for concern when promiscuous stocking leads to loss of the integrity of unique
gene pools in established wild populations. It also suggests that deci-
sions relating to stocking policy should be made by biologists not
burdened by political considerations.

Hatcheries are necessary if trout fishing, on the scale now practiced, is to continue. Streams in which natural reproduction is insufficient to allow for the presence of self-sustaining populations might
nevertheless allow survival, and therefore function as trout streams, if
periodic stocking were to be practiced. And this practice would obviously relieve fishing pressure on natural populations elsewhere.

If waters to be stocked are uninhabited by trout but apparently
capable of supporting reproducing trout populations, a huge, fast-
growing hatchery strain of a suitable species might be a better choice
for introduction than a wild strain. It is a general biological principle
that the selection of favorable traits (genes) proceeds more rapidly
when there has been an introduction into new environmental conditions. This is because the new environment, different in many ways
than the environment from which the introduced individuals came, ex-
erts some different demands. And the principle applies whether wild or
hatchery trout are introduced. So why not use a strain bred for superior
size and growth rate? In either case, after a number of generations
natural selection would provide a gene pool superior, in terms of the
new environmental demands, than the gene pool of the originally introduced fish.

Selection that occurs in hatcheries is not always "artificial."
Highly disease-resistant strains have been produced by exposing large
numbers of trout to disease agents and, after the majority has suc-
cumbed, using the few survivors as breeding stock. In essence, this constitutes natural selection. Certainly it's not the subjective eye of the
hatchery personnel that chooses the survivors. The same process has
also given rise to trout better able to withstand life in waters attaining
temperatures near the upper limits of tolerance. In this case, large

numbers of fish have been exposed to high temperatures, with brood fish being chosen from those surviving the ordeal. Though costly in terms of trout, this method yields the desired result as no other method would.

Chromosomes, Genes, and the Mechanism of Heredity

Genes determine hereditary traits. They are chemical units located on chromosomes — structures found in virtually all cells of the body. Each species has a fixed number of chromosomes per cell, which is called its "chromosome count."[1] Chromosomes occur in matched pairs. When a rainbow trout, for instance, is said to have a chromosome count of 60, it means that there are 30 pairs. And in all cells of the body — muscle cells, liver cells, etc. — the chromosomes are essentially identical in appearance. If there are two of each kind of chromosome, and if genes are located on chromosomes, it follows that each cell has two of each "kind" of gene. Hereditary traits, then, are determined by gene pairs.

When sex cells are produced by testes and ovaries, the sperm and eggs that result possess only one of each chromosome pair. So in rainbows, with their normal chromosome count of 60, eggs and sperm have only 30 chromosomes each. With respect to genes, each member of a gene pair passes into a separate sex cell. Clearly, the union of any given egg with a sperm cell during spawning would bring the chromosome count up to 60 again, and the resulting offspring would be determined insofar as genetic characters are concerned.

Genetic traits are so numerous that it's impossible for anyone, in crossing a pair of fish, to keep tabs on all of them. But to illustrate the hereditary mechanism a single trait can be selected and its pattern of inheritance followed. An obvious characteristic, such as albinism, the lack of normal pigmentation (Figure 2.1, color photo, p. 38), would be most suitable.

In rainbow trout there is a gene pair responsible for the expression of coloration, and in most normally colored rainbows both genes of the pair dictate that the color be normal. In some trout, however, one of the genes may dictate albinism. Such trout are still normally colored, because the gene for normal coloration is dominant over the gene for albinism and masks the latter's effect.

---

1. Sometimes there are variations in chromosome counts within a species, as in the cutthroat trout (mentioned earlier), but such instances are rare.

It is customary to indicate a dominant gene with a capital letter (N for normal) and a recessive gene that might occur with it in a pair by the same letter, but not capitalized (n for albinism in this instance). Normally colored rainbows, then, can either have both genes for normal coloration (NN), or one gene for normal coloration and one gene for albinism (Nn). Only if both genes are for albinism (nn) will a trout actually be albino.

Figure 2.2 shows a cross between a normal trout (NN) and an albino (nn). Because all of the sex cells of the normal trout will carry a gene N, while all of the sex cells produced by the albino will have an n, every one of their offspring will be Nn and will therefore be normally colored. When these offspring are mature and ready to spawn, all of them will produce sex cells, half of which carry an N gene and half of which carry an n. And any two fish from this generation, if crossed, will yield a subsequent generation in which about 25 percent of the offspring are albino.

When eggs and sperm are released en masse during the spawning act they tumble about in the turbulent water above the nest, mixing in a random manner. Which sperm fertilizes which egg is a matter of pure chance, like flipping coins, and chance, in this case, will give a 3:1 ratio of normal trout to albinos.

If you visualize a typical stream situation — with resident trout and some sort of trout predator — you can see how certain genes can be selected for in populations. Under most conditions albinos would be more visible to predators and therefore more prone to capture. Since fewer albinos would survive to reproduce, the number of albino genes in the population's gene pool would decrease. By contrast, the normal genes, which confer a more protective coloration, would tend to increase.

The genes controlling countless traits in any population are determined in the same way. Unique environments favor certain genes over others and produce, over time, gene pools peculiarly well adapted to local conditions. That's why such a high premium is placed on native strains. If a load of hatchery fish — or even wild fish from another environment — are dumped into a body of water and allowed to interbreed with natives, a unique gene pool — a unique strain — is lost.

There are absolutely legions of genes being passed from one generation to another, but it is not always the case that one member of a gene pair will completely dominate the other. A color variant of the rainbow trout, known as the "golden rainbow" — not to be confused with the golden trout (*Salmo aguabonita*) — is lacking in melanin, a dark

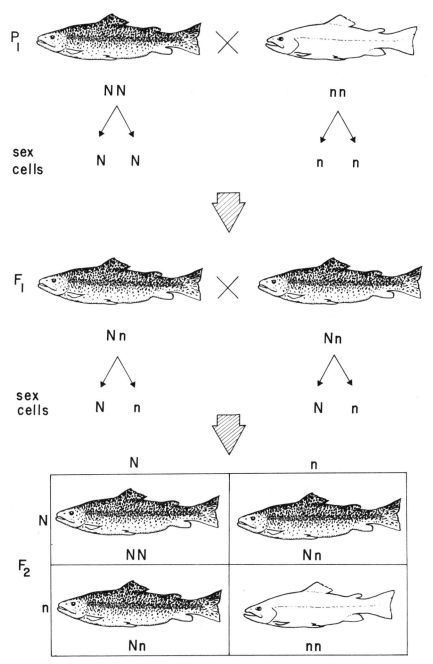

Figure 2.2. A monohybrid cross between an albino rainbow trout and a rainbow possessing two genes for normal coloration. P_1 refers to the parental generation. The first generation of offspring, also called the first filial generation, is indicated by F_1. And the following generation, the second filial generation, is indicated by F_2. F_2 genetic makeup: NN = 25%, Nn = 50%, nn = 25%. F_2 physical appearance: normal = 75%, albino = 25%.

pigment. Such a trout is gold with typically dark eyes, and with evidence of the rainbow stripe along the lateral line (Figure 2.3, second from top, color photo, p. 39). The gene responsible for this "color dilution" is neither dominant nor recessive to the gene for normal color, so in order to have the golden color a trout must have both genes of the pair for gold. If a fish has one gene for normal coloration and one for gold, its coloration will be intermediate between normal and golden — what hatcherymen call a "palomino" (Figure 2.3, bottom, color photo, p. 39). A cross between a normal and a golden rainbow produces all palomino offspring (Figure 2.4); and two palomino parents will yield normal, palomino, and golden offspring in a 1:2:1 ratio.

Some inherited traits are determined by many gene pairs instead of just one pair, which permits a broad spectrum of physical types instead of the either-or situation associated with the single gene pair. If enough counts are made in a population of characters such as body length or egg production, some high values are found, some low ones, and a concentration of values clustered around an average. Environmental influences do bear on traits like these, but even if the environmental effect can be minimized or done away with a normal distribution will be evident, indicating that many gene pairs are involved.

Some traits may be enhanced, modified, or masked by the sex of an individual (i.e., its hormones). The hook or "kype" that develops on the jaws of mature male salmonids is such a sex-influenced character, and so is the difference in spawning coloration between the sexes.

In recent years, much genetic work on trout has dealt with biochemical characters. Most of these traits aren't of the sort that can be spotted by looking at a fish, but rather have to be tested for with special laboratory procedures. On the other hand, knowledge of them is highly desirable because they aren't influenced by environmental conditions, as are some of the more obvious characters like color. For example, different stocks of the same trout species may have different molecular variations in certain body proteins. In the laboratory, a "genetic profile" of biochemical characters may be constructed for a stock; the basic idea is comparable to blood typing, but the procedure utilizes a much broader range of body proteins, rather than blood proteins alone. With such a technique available, a biologist can determine the stock to which a trout (for example) of unknown origin belongs. The practical uses of this kind of technique include identifying the origins of migratory fish, detecting inbreeding, and determining the success of plantings of different stocks in the same body of water.

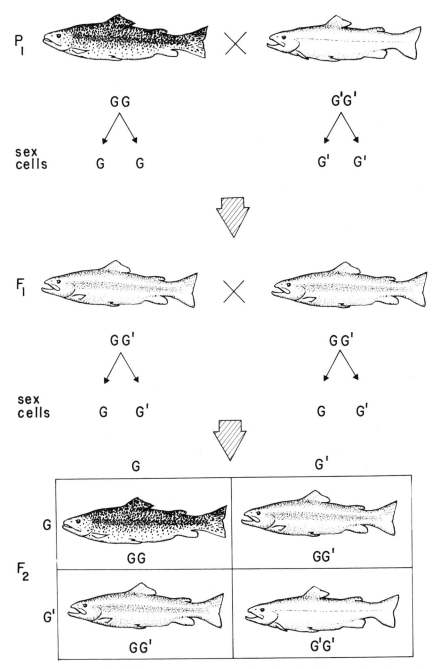

Figure 2.4. A monohybrid cross between a normally colored rainbow and a golden rainbow. G indicates a gene for normal coloration, while G′ indicates a gene for golden color. Because neither gene masks the effect of the other (i.e., because there is incomplete dominance), individuals with both kinds of genes are intermediate in appearance between individuals having both genes of the same kind. These intermediate individuals are called palominos. F_2 genetic makeup: GG = 25%, GG′ = 50%, G′G′ = 25%. F_2 physical appearance: normal = 25%, palomino = 50%, golden = 25%.

Species Hybrids

It would be natural enough for biologists to cross different species for no other reason than to see what might turn up. But there's also interest in the possibility of using hybrids as special hatchery breeding stock. The idea is to determine whether, in some cases, it might be practical to backcross fertile hybrids with parent species and, in the process, transfer desirable traits from one species to another without a significant loss of species identity. It would be beneficial from the standpoint of the fisheries biologist, for example, if the size and longevity of the lake trout could be bred into the brook trout, or if resistance to the disease furunculosis — a trait of rainbows — could be transferred to browns or brookies.

Another possibility offered by hybrids is for stocking programs. Unique appearance, fighting quality and habitat utilization might make a given hybrid not only a desirable game fish, but also a useful entity for efficient use of certain waters.

It has been known for centuries that some species of salmonids may hybridize. By the late nineteenth century, a number of experimental crossings had taken place or were in progress in England and Europe, as well as in New York State, and some concrete results were beginning to accumulate. That the results were quite variable for some crossings can be attributed to many factors, including variations in the genetic makeup of the parent fish and the physical conditions under which the experiments were performed.

One of the most often cited of recent hybridization studies was conducted from 1952 to 1955 at the Benner Springs Research Station in Pennsylvania. Since the species involved would be of interest to North American anglers, some of the results are shown in Table 2.1.

Whereas trout of the same species have similar chromosomes, this isn't necessarily the case for trout of different species, and chromosome similarity is normally necessary in order for two individuals to produce offspring. Chromosome counts for the species used in the Benner Springs experiments ranged from 60 (for rainbows) to 84 (for the chars). There is no information on how the chromosomes of any one species compare with those of another, and all that can be said is that a certain degree of chromosome compatability must exist if viable hybrid offspring are to result.

Different species have their own incubation periods. At a water temperature of 50° F, the rainbow trout's incubation period (from fertilization to hatching) is up to 10 days shorter than that for most other

Figure 1.1. Typical cutthroats of the interior, showing characteristic large spots. (Courtesy of George Sura and Robert Toulouse of *Wyoming Wildlife.*)

Figure 1.2. A cutthroat of the Snake River strain, showing the many small spots which readily distinguish it from other interior strains and which give it an appearance similar to that of coastal cutthroats. (Courtesy of Keith Bilby.)

Figure 1.3. A male Lahontan cutthroat. (Courtesy of Dale Lockard, Nevada Department of Fish and Game.)

Figure 1.5. A Colorado greenback cutthroat trout from Como Creek. (Courtesy of Keith Bilby.)

Figure 1.6. A California golden trout from the South Fork of the Kern River. (Courtesy of Leonard Fisk, California Department of Fish and Game.)

Figure 1.7. The gila trout. (Photo by H. J. McKirdy. Published by permission of R. E. Swigart, U.S. Forest Service.)

Figure 1.8. A red-banded trout. (Courtesy of Leonard Fisk, California Department of Fish and Game.)

Figure 1.12. The Sunapee trout. (Copyright National Geographic Society.)

Figure 1.14. An old (date unknown) photo of the aurora trout. It appears this form is now extinct. (Courtesy of Dr. W. B. Scott, Curator, Royal Ontario Museum.)

Figure 2.1. An albino rainbow trout and a trout of normal coloration. (Courtesy of the *Journal of Heredity*.)

Figure 2.3. The top fish is a rare "chimera" with both normal tissue and golden rainbow tissue. Below it is a golden rainbow. Third from the top is a normally colored rainbow, and at the bottom a palomino trout, a cross between a golden rainbow and a normally colored rainbow. (Courtesy of Dr. James Wright, Pennsylvania State University.)

Figure 2.6. Splake. (Courtesy of Vernon Hacker, Wisconsin Department of Natural Resources.)

Figure 2.7. A tiger trout. (Courtesy of Russell Daly, Wisconsin Department of Natural Resources.)

40

Table 2.1. The results of hybridization experiments published by Buss and Wright (1956). When a cross is expressed (e.g., brown × brook) the female parent is given first. Chromosome number is given in parentheses.

	Female Parent	Male Parent	Number of Eggs Incubated	Eggs Eyed	Number of Eggs Hatched	Number of Surviving Fry	% of Surviving Fry
1.	Brown trout (80)	Brook trout (84)	100,000	Yes	65,000	4,000	4.00
2.	Brook trout (84)	Brown trout (80)	4,467	Yes	128	22	.50
3.	Rainbow trout (60)	Brook trout (84)	1,130	Yes	610	7	.60
4.	Brook trout (84)	Rainbow trout (60)	18,014	Yes	0	0	.00
5.	Rainbow trout (60)	Brown trout (80)	3,380	Yes	1,825	40	1.20
6.	Brown trout (80)	Rainbow trout (60)	5,662	Yes	0	0	.00
7.	Brook trout (84)	Lake trout (84)	29,687	Yes	261	217	.70
8.	Lake trout (84)	Brook trout (84)	30,319	Yes	9,782	8,500	28.00
9.	Brown trout (80)	Lake trout (84)	2,617	Yes	143	2	.08
10.	Rainbow trout (60)	Lake trout (84)	1,660	Yes	3	0	.00
11.	Brown trout (80)	Landlocked salmon (60)	2,400	Yes	685	8	.30
12.	Brown trout (80)	Splake (84) (lake × brook)	3,337	Yes	948	107	3.20
13.	Splake (84) (lake × brook)	Brown trout (80)	2,814	Yes	9	0	.00
14.	Brook trout (84)	Tiger trout (?) (brown × brook)	628	No	0	0	.00
15.	Brown trout (80)	Tiger trout (?) (brown × brook)	3,795	No	0	0	.00
16.	Brook trout (84)	Splake (84) (lake × brook)	5,507	Yes	3,371	2,844	51.60
17.	Splake (84) (lake × brook)	Brook trout (84)	2,233	Yes	209	176	7.90
18.	Splake (84) (lake × brook)	Splake (84) (lake × brook)	51,740	Yes	?	5,146	10.00
19.	Brook trout (84)	A cross between (?) a splake and a brook trout ([lake × brook] × brook)	3,146	Yes	2,575	2,514	79.90

The number of eggs hatching may be misleading if not related to similar values from normal crosses, since even in normal crosses eggs are lost. Loss of eggs prior to hatching is referred to as "pickoff" by hatcherymen. For purposes of comparison, authors Buss and Wright gave average pickoff values of 25% for brown trout, 33% for brook trout, and 40% for rainbows.

salmonids. In general, there is a better chance for the production of healthy hybrid offspring in cases where the two parent species have similar incubation periods. For maximum success, eggs should be taken from the parent with the shorter incubation period. Egg size is also crucial, and the female parent should be of the species with the larger eggs. Apparently the mere physical confinement of a small egg can lead to deformities in offspring, especially in the tail region.

If a given cross yields hybrid offspring of a certain physical appearance, offspring of the reciprocal cross may appear quite different. The hybrid commonly known as the "tiger trout," for example, results from the fertilization of brown trout eggs with the milt of brook trout. The reciprocal cross (brook trout female × brown trout male) yields offspring which, though sometimes called "tiger trout" (less frequently "leopard trout"), are quite different in shape and their pattern of vermiculation from the more common brown × brook hybrids. No explanation can be offered, since the mechanics of genetic control of such species hybrids hasn't been elucidated.

Not surprisingly, many crosses, especially those resulting in exceedingly low percentages of surviving fry, yield a sizable number of malformed individuals, cripples, and "monsters." In some crosses two-headed fry are common (Figure 2.5). Since the process of embryonic development is essentially genetically determined, and because under normal conditions the process depends upon the occurrence of chromosomes from parents of the same species, any chromosome incompatabilities are apt to give rise to changes in biochemical reactions; these, in turn, may be made evident by various deformities.

Theoretically, the more closely related two species are, the more successful an attempt at their hybridization should be. Accordingly, greater difficulty should (theoretically) be experienced when crossing chars (*Salvelinus*) with trout (*Salmo*) than when crossing two species of the same genus.

A perusal of Table 2.1 will show that most potential hybrids don't offer much promise, if for no other reason than that their survival is so low. The so-called "brownbow" (rainbow × brown), once thought of as a potentially useful hybrid, is no longer considered seriously. Of the many hybrids studied, only two have been worthy of widespread consideration for stocking programs — the splake (lake trout × brook trout) and the tiger trout (brown trout × brook trout).

The Splake
There's little doubt that the splake (Figure 2.6, color photo, p. 40) is the most successful of the hybrid salmonids. First generation splake are fer-

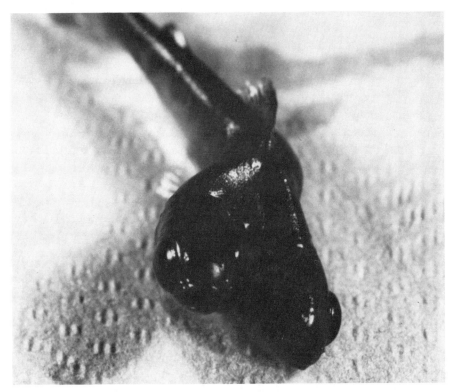

Figure 2.5. Two-headed fry are not uncommon in some crosses. The parentage of this specimen isn't known. (Photo by Steve Whitman.)

tile, and long-term breeding experiments have gone at least as far as four generations. Splake grow more rapidly than either brookies or lake trout when placed in similar conditions, and they also have a greater tendency to school than either parent.

Like both parents, the splake is a fall spawner, but whereas brookies normally carry on their reproductive activities during the day and lakers spawn primarily by night, splake are active around the clock. Splake have been observed spawning on sandy bottoms, like brook trout, as well as on talus slopes, like lake trout. They resemble brook trout with respect to the duration of their spawning activity, which tends to be long, perhaps in the neighborhood of five or six weeks.

Even though they grow rapidly, splake have the attribute of early maturation; nearly all are mature by the age of three. This trait in concert with the fact that they prefer shallower water than do lake trout, made them a natural choice for stocking in the Great Lakes when the lamprey, which parasitizes fish, became established. Lampreys, like lake trout, are characteristically deep water inhabitants, and they show a distinct preference for large hosts on the order of 20 inches or more. In the Great Lakes, lake trout don't spawn until they are about 24 inches in length, long after having become fair game for lampreys. In the same region, splake first spawn at about 15 or 16 inches, before becoming prime targets for lampreys, and their preference for shallow water keeps them relatively secure from attack.

Splake have all the earmarks of a fine game fish. Most anglers report that a hybrid on the end of a line reacts more like a brook trout than a lake trout, and "mark and return" surveys show that splake are often more easily caught than either parent species.

The Tiger Trout

The tiger is a real anomaly. Since the female parent, a brown trout, belongs to the genus *Salmo,* and the male parent is a brook trout — a char and thus in the genus *Salvelinus* — the offspring is not only a cross between different species but between different genera (Figure 2.7, color photo, p. 40). To date no one has succeeded in determining the chromosome count of this hybrid.

In the Benner Springs breeding experiments about 65 percent of the fertilized eggs hatched — a figure roughly comparable to what would be expected from a normal brook trout mating, and about 10 percent less than the average expectancy for a normal brown trout cross. However, the figures for fry survival in two different hybrid experiments were only 4 and 5 percent respectively (for the results of one of these experiments, see Table 2.1, mating 1). After hatching, a white spot develops on the yolk sac of most sac fry, which enlarges as the process of yolk absorption progresses. The death of these fry inevitably results. No disease-producing microorganisms have ever been found, so the disorder is widely considered to be a result of biochemical disturbances arising from genetic incompatability.

Attempts by a variety of breeders to produce tiger offspring have yielded fry survival figures of from 0 to 36 percent. Because different strains within a species vary genetically from one another, the varying results of crossing experiments may well be attributed largely to the strains from which parent fish are chosen. At its Wild Rose Hatchery, the state of Wisconsin has been getting tiger-fry survival figures of from 10 to 25 percent. In one year an estimated 35,000 to 40,000 tiger trout in the six-inch class were raised from an initial 250,000 fertilized eggs. Some biologists believe that one of the secrets of high fry survival lies in the use of a female from a large strain and a male from a small strain.

The tiger trout is as striking as any fish that swims. Though a few are pale, the majority exhibit a vivid pattern of "chain mail" vermiculations. The red belly typical of brook trout males is generally expressed in tigers as yellow orange. The scales of the hybrid are large, as in *Salmo*. Even though their secondary sexual characters (general build, shape of the jaw, vividness of coloration in males, etc.) are usually quite obvious, tiger trout are sterile.

Most reports suggest that tigers are willing risers and superb fighters, exhibiting a greater tendency to jump than either parent. Stomach analyses of stream-resident tiger trout indicate that they are strongly inclined to feed on insects, and in waters where they are found in cohabitation with rainbows and brown trout, tigers may sometimes be found feeding at the surface when the other fish are down.

It appears that most introductions of tiger trout have been made exclusively for the sake of novelty, but the potential offered by this hybrid is also being put to practical use in the Great Lakes. In recent years, brown trout have contributed in a big way to sport fishing in Lake Michigan. However, mortalities are exceedingly high in browns spawning for the first time (at age three or four), since spawning stress makes them prone to a fungus infection. It has been reported that mortality resulting from fungus infection is virtually 100 percent among such fish in spawning areas along western Lake Michigan. An obvious consequence is that these fish never have an opportunity to grow larger than they are at age three or four. A program proposed by Wisconsin would involve the stocking of tiger trout in the hope that the hybrid's lack of reproductive urge, and hence the lack of stress, would avert high mortalities and allow for larger fish.

Genetics and evolution are intimately intertwined. Fundamentally, it is the genetic makeup that defines a species, so the forces that select for or against certain genes generation after generation will determine the evolutionary direction a species takes. For trout that are wild and have existed for long periods in relatively stable conditions, it is safe to assume that the preponderance of genes favor survival in the wild, or else natural selection would have long since done away with them. For strains that have undergone long periods of domestication, no such assumption can be made. But even though the use of domestic strains often warrants caution, the breeding of salmonids is a major branch of pisciculture. States produce hordes of trout for the growing numbers of anglers, commercial raisers supply a thriving market, and at least two species hybrids are of value in some situations. Hatchery-bred fish will continue to have a major role in the North American fishing scene.

3.

The Salmonid Body

> The trout is a fish highly valued both in this and foreign nations. He may
> be justly said, as the old poet said of wine, and we English say of
> venison, to be a generous fish.   —IZAAC WALTON, 1676

A trout is essentially a collection of interdependent systems. Most of
the systems are easily exposed, and a fairly decent dissection of a foot-
long fish can be done at streamside with nothing more than a penknife.
Brown trout were the fish most readily available to me, so the diagrams
and photos in this chapter are of browns, but as far as basic anatomy is
concerned all salmonid species are pretty much the same.

External Features

A trout body, torpedo-shaped and tapering at both ends, is ideal for
presenting a minimum of resistance to water flow. It is divided into
three distinct regions: head, trunk, and tail (Figure 3.1). The head,
which lacks scales, extends from the nose to the back of the gill covers.
For the most part the gill covers consist of bone with a thin covering of
flesh, but their lower parts are the thin branchiostegal membranes supported by a number of bony branchiostegal rays. Counts of these rays,
like scale counts and fin ray counts, are frequently used by biologists in
distinguishing different salmonid species and populations from one
another.

The trunk extends from the head back to the vent. In front of the
belly it connects to the head by a long, tapering extension called the
isthmus, which can be seen between the branchiostegal membranes.
Between the vent and the end of the caudal fin is the tail or caudal
region; the caudal peduncle is that portion between the anal fin and the
front of the caudal fin.

All fins but one are made of tough membrane supported by bony
fin rays. Salmonids are among the soft-rayed fish — the rays are jointed
and therefore flexible. Most rays are branched. The caudal fin, which

46

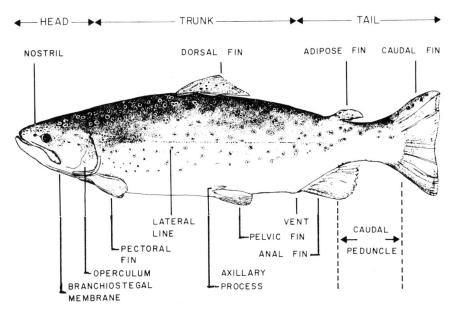

Figure 3.1. External features of trout.

may be smaller in hatchery than in wild fish because of frequent abrasion on troughs, is moved in the horizontal plane by the body musculature to push the fish forward. The anal fin, frequently used (especially by spawning females) to gather information about the substrate, is also located far back enough to assist in forward propulsion. (A well-meaning sportswriter once suggested clipping off the anal fins of trout and returning the fish to the water, the idea being that the fins would serve as trophies and the fish spared. In light of the fact that the fin isn't useless, its removal would place a trout at a competitive disadvantage, and could make spawning impossible for a female. And the exposure of underlying tissue always makes fungal and bacterial infection much more likely.) The anal fin, along with the dorsal fin, also helps keep the body upright and on its chosen course. The second dorsal fin, or adipose fin, is fleshy, is not rayed, and, as far as we know, is without particular function, although it may serve to balance the asymmetry of the dorsal and anal fins.

The paired fins, the pectorals, and pelvics, are especially useful in balancing, maneuvering, turning, and braking. The pelvic fins of many game fish tend to be closer to the pectorals than they are in trout, where they're located in the middle of the body. At the base of each pelvic fin is an elongated axillary process, actually a modified scale.

The outermost layer of the skin, the epidermis, is very thin, is well-endowed with mucous glands, has an abundance of pigmented cells and covers the scales (Figure 3.2). Below the epidermis lies the thicker, tougher dermis which, in addition to pigmented cells, contains nerves, blood vessels, fibrous connective tissue (to which the skin owes its toughness), and the scales. Trout have the cycloid type of scale, which is essentially a bony disc devoid of spines (Figure 3.3). Each lies in a pocket of dermis with only a small part visible, the rest being overlain by the scales just in front of it. Scales along the lateral line are pierced with holes leading into the lateral line system.

Bone in scales is laid down in concentric rings (circuli). During the winter, when growth is retarded, circuli tend to be crowded together, and there may even be some reabsorption at the margin of a scale. In this way annual lines (annuli) are formed which may be read to determine age. Adult sea-run salmon put on no growth while in fresh water; this leaves a "spawning mark" on a scale.

Bones composing the margins of the upper and lower jaws bear sharp teeth, as do other bones in the roof of the mouth. And the tongue has a double row of teeth. In older males, the lower jaw develops a hook, the kype. If you look just inside the mouth, along the edges, you'll see flaps of tissue that act as valves in preventing a backflow of water during respiration.

The eyes have no lids, but are covered by a thin layer of

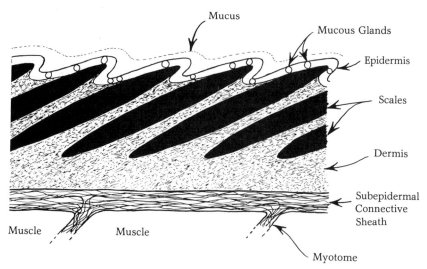

Figure 3.2. Section through the skin: a diagrammatic representation.

Figure 3.3. Cycloid scales. The scales in this series were taken from brown trout of the Pigeon River in Michigan's Otsego County. What appear as dark concentric circles are the circuli. Roman numerals indicate annuli and, hence, the age of the fish. (Photo by the Wisconsin Department of Natural Resources, Madison, Wisconsin.)

transparent skin. Each nostril has both a front opening and a back opening. The opening in front is guarded by a flap of tissue which directs water through that opening and into the olfactory sac, the pouch housing the ultrasensitive organ of smell. Because there's no connection between the olfactory sac and the mouth (you can determine the extent of the sac by probing with something blunt) water simply passes out of the back opening of the nostril. So there's a continuous flow through the sac as a trout moves along — or as stream water runs by a stationary trout. Either way, the fish has a sensitive monitoring device for chemicals in the water passing over its body.

Just in front of the anal fin there are two openings, together called the vent (Figure 3.4). The more forward of the two, the anus, marks the terminus of the intestinal tract. The other is the urogenital opening through which urine and either eggs or sperm pass; it leads into a chamber containing a fleshy swelling, the urogenital papilla, on which the tiny genital opening and the urinary opening, also very small, are located. The papilla itself can vary quite a bit in size. It is largest during the spawning season, when it may be seen protruding from the urogenital opening.

The Respiratory System

The respiratory system's primary function is getting oxygen into the body of the beast — oxygen needed for metabolism — and simultaneously getting rid of some waste products, notably carbon dioxide.

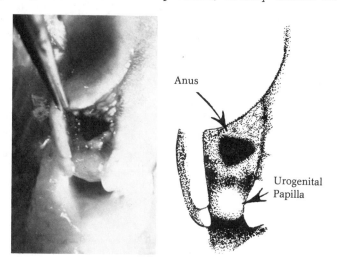

Anus

Urogenital
Papilla

Figure 3.4. The region of the vent (this specimen is a female). Forceps are seen holding aside a flap of the body wall. (Photo by Steve Whitman.)

Salmonids, as a group, are characteristic of waters well supplied with dissolved oxygen, and this oxygen they take in through the gills.

The mechanical process of respiration is a complex of beautifully coordinated movements carried out by muscles of the mouth and gill covers. During each respiratory cycle a volume of water enters the mouth, passes through the gill chambers (in which the gills are located), and leaves through the crescent-shaped gill openings at the back of the head. The gill covers act as valves by allowing only the exit of water from the gill chambers; their soft membranous edges allow them to fit snugly to the body. Mechanical respiration goes on constantly and, as in the case of air-breathers, its rate becomes more rapid as the need of the body for oxygen increases.

By lifting a gill cover you can expose a gill chamber, and see within it five gill arches, four of which are equipped with a double row of delicate filaments along their back edges. In living trout the filaments are bright red because the blood in them is visible through the incredibly thin tissue. As blood courses through the filaments, a mere few thousandths of an inch of gill tissue separates it from water passing through the gill chamber; such a thin separation allows dissolved oxygen to diffuse into the blood even as wastes diffuse out (Figure 3.5).

Just inside each gill cover is a pseudobranch, or false gill (Figure 3.6), the exact function of which isn't known. Some biologists suggest that it may have a secretory or sensory role.

Located on the forward edges of the gill arches are the comblike gill rakers, which act as strainers to prevent large particles of food from washing out over the delicate gill filaments. The whole mouth-gill area is rather like a sieve. Fish that feed by filtering tiny particles from water typically possess numerous long, thin rakers, but salmonids have the shorter, thicker rakers characteristic of species that feed on larger prey.

The Skeletal System

The skeletal system acts as a framework for the rest of the body. In salmonids it includes such a multitude of hair-fine bones that it would be virtually impossible to construct a decent mounted skeleton. As an alternative, I have had an X-ray made of an intact 22-inch brown trout, carefully skinned so the scales wouldn't cast shadows that would obscure the deeper bones (Figure 3.7).

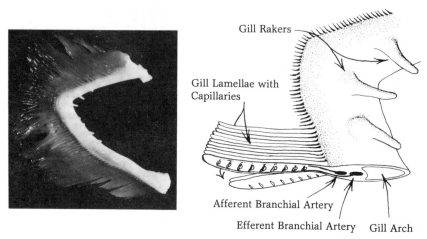

Figure 3.5. The photo is of a gill arch from the right side of a brown trout. The drawing shows a portion of the arch with some of its principal parts. The afferent branchial artery carries blood into the gill. It is at the gill lamellae, the delicate, capillary-filled extensions, that gas transfer (oxygen and carbon dioxide) between blood and water takes place. The efferent branchial artery carries freshly oxygenated blood out of the gill and to the body. (Photo by Steve Whitman.)

Figure 3.6. The gill chamber and pharynx, with the pseudobranch appearing as a dark spot on the upper wall of the gill chamber. (Photo by Steve Whitman.)

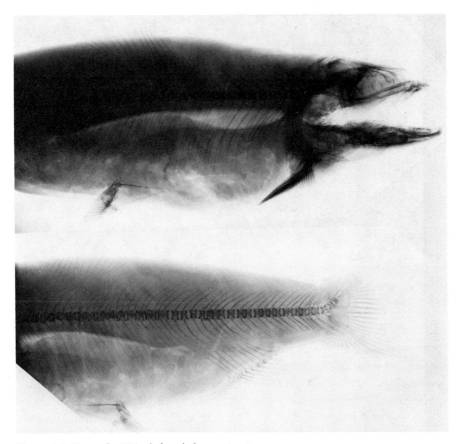

Figure 3.7. X-ray of a 22-inch female brown trout.

The trout skeleton is constructed primarily of bone, but it does have some cartilage components. It can be thought of as having three main subdivisions. One is the axial skeleton, so named because it follows the long axis of the body; it consists of the upper part of the skull (the part housing the brain) and the vertebral column. The visceral skeleton is made up of the jaws, the elements suspending the jaws, and the five pairs of gill arches; by and large, it is involved with eating and respiration. The appendicular skeleton is associated with the appendages; its principle structures are the two girdles that support the paired fins (pectoral and pelvic), but the bony rays of the median fins are included too.

The trout skull isn't static with respect to shape. Throughout the life of an individual different portions of the structure grow at dissimilar rates, so that there are variations in shape among the skulls

Figure 3.8. The kype, seen as a recurved hook at the tip of the lower jaw. The fish is a male brown trout. (Photo by Steve Whitman.)

of trout of different ages. Superimposed upon the changes resulting from age are changes associated with spawning, such as the kype that develops in males where the bones of the lower jaw come together (Figure 3.8).

Much of the skull is actually composed of cartilage, but this part is normally deeper and hidden from view by more superficial bones. Early in the life of a trout the cartilage of the skull is formed; thereafter, hard bones are added. But even though bones develop many cartilage parts persist, so the skull never really becomes a solid bone structure.

Beginning at the back of the skull and running the length of the body is the vertebral column. The number of vertebrae in salmonids ranges from 54 to 56 for brown trout (individual variations exist) up to about 72 for chinook salmon. The central portion of each vertebra is shaped like a cylinder, and the upper part of each vertebra is in the form of a bony arch through which the spinal cord, which runs the length of the vertebral column, passes (Figure 3.9). Vertebrae in the hind part of the body also have an arch on the lower surface where blood vessels pass through. In the trunk region, where the large body cavity is located just below the vertebral column, these lower arches aren't found.

Trout, like many other fish, are equipped with an abundance of very thin bones. Extending off of the vertebral arches — upper and lower — there are long spines sandwiched in the median plane of the body between the right and left halves. Some of the spines have divided ends. Coming off the lower sides of the vertebrae, where the vertebral column spans the large body cavity, there are extremely fine bones called pleural ribs. These lie between the body musculature and the thin lining of the body cavity. More bones of similar delicacy are found within the muscle tissue of the upper part of the body; they show up fairly well in the X-ray.

The hindmost extremity of the skeleton is modified in salmonids in such a way that the last three vertebrae are bent upward. The lower spines of these three vertebrae, rather than being thin projections, are very broad and together form a vertical sheet of bone to which are attached the rays of the caudal fin (Figure 3.10). The external symmetry of the tail is deceptive, since it really derives from the lower side of the vertebral column.

Supporting all fins except the adipose are the fin rays, which are jointed and, for the most part, branched. Each of the tiny jointed units has two component parts one on the right side and one on the left (Figure 3.11). At the base of a ray the halves are separated so that what amounts to a split end is formed. In the dorsal and anal fins the split end of each ray fits over a tiny spherical bone, which is one of a set of three bones supporting the ray. The innermost of the three is long and thin and, like many of the other very slender bones in the trout, is embedded between the body muscles of the right and left halves. In the

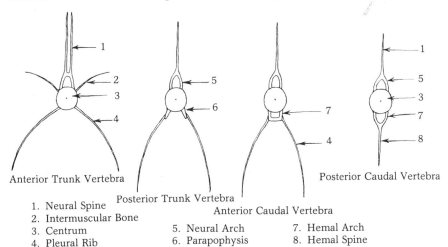

Anterior Trunk Vertebra

Posterior Trunk Vertebra

Anterior Caudal Vertebra

Posterior Caudal Vertebra

1. Neural Spine
2. Intermuscular Bone
3. Centrum
4. Pleural Rib

5. Neural Arch
6. Parapophysis

7. Hemal Arch
8. Hemal Spine

Figure 3.9. Typical vertebrae of the trout. (After Parker and Haswell, 1963.)

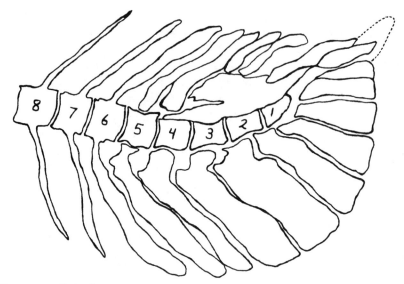

Figure 3.10. Skeletal structure of the caudal region. (After Norden, 1961.)

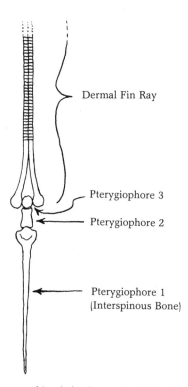

Dermal Fin Ray

Pterygiophore 3

Pterygiophore 2

Pterygiophore 1
(Interspinous Bone)

Figure 3.11. A dermal fin ray and its skeletal supports. (After Parker and Haswell, 1963.)

X-ray they appear at first glance to be internal continuations of the fin rays. The split ends of caudal fin rays fit over the edges of the vertical sheet of bone at the end of the vertebral column.

The pectoral girdle, which corresponds to the shoulder region in humans, supports the pectoral fins. It consists of nine paired bones attached by ligaments to the skull. The pelvic girdle, represented in man by the hip region, is very reduced in trout, consisting only of a pair of L-shaped bones. Rather than articulating with some other part of the skeleton, they are buried within the musculature of the body. Both the pectoral and pelvic fins have rays similar in construction to the rays of the median fins.

The Muscular System

The function of muscle tissue is to contract, thereby making something — whatever the muscle is attached to — move. Most of the muscle in a salmonid is in the great masses that extend on either side of the body from the back of the head to the caudal fin, and which are responsible for swimming activity. The filets, if you wish.

If you skin one side of a trout you can see that the muscles there are segmentally arranged (Figure 3.12). Each segment is in the form of a zigzag, rather like a W on its side. Between muscle segments there are thin sheets of connective tissue, and it is to these sheets that the muscle fibers in each segment actually attach. When any given muscle segment contracts, it brings two sheets of connective tissue closer together, and therefore causes a slight local bend in the body. If all of this body musculature was in the form of a homogeneous mass rather than in segments, the contraction of muscles on one side would simply cause the body to describe a uniform arc from head to tail. This would result in nothing more than a thrashing action that wouldn't do much at all to move the body through water. As it is, swimming is accomplished by the propagation of waves along the body, from front to back, by the serial contraction of the muscle segments.

The zigzag shape of these segments isn't just a superficial trait. The W is even more accentuated deeper in the muscle, closer to the vertebral column, so that each segment is somewhat cone-shaped (Figure 3.12). Through this design action of a given muscle segment is spread over a greater length of the body than would be the case were it simply a vertical sheet. It's an efficient arrangement.

As a trout embryo is developing, portions of muscle separate from the great segmented mass and develop into groups of muscles

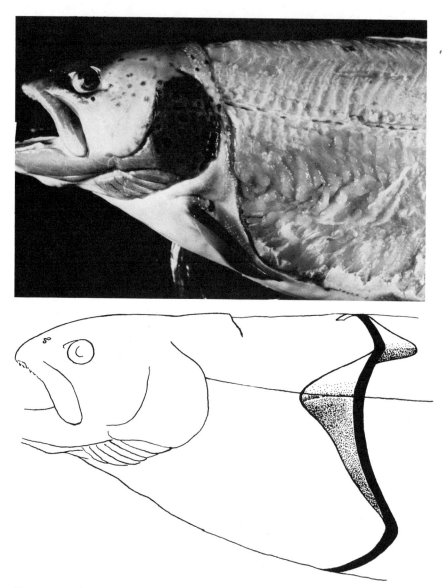

Figure 3.12. The photo shows muscle segments (myotomes) and the connective tissue sheets separating them (myosepta). The drawing shows an isolated myotome. The blackened area represents that portion which is exposed in a skinned fish. More deeply, the myotome extends along a greater length of the body. (Photo by Steve Whitman.)

with highly specific functions. Many muscles in the head are involved with the complex acts of operating the jaws and gills. In the midline, top and bottom, there are longitudinal muscles which flex the body in the vertical plane. But the lateral flexibility of a fish is greater than its vertical flexibility, and in order to make a sharp vertical turn the common maneuver is to turn first on the side and then to bend laterally. Each fin is equipped with numerous muscles, many quite small, that are responsible for erecting or flattening the fin or for accomplishing the multitude of actions the fin is capable of carrying out.

In a freshly made cross section through a trout you can see that some muscle closer to the skin is distinctly darker than the deeper muscle (Figure 3.13). In dark muscle there is a larger proportion of blood to contractile elements; in light muscle there is a greater proportion of contractile elements and a corresponding lower percentage of blood. Dark muscle is associated with prolonged activity of a routine nature, such as that required for holding a position in a moderate current. But when sudden action and all-out exertion are called for, it's light muscle that's used. Because of a relatively poorer blood supply, however, light muscle activity can't be sustained for long periods.

Quite aside from this light muscle-dark muscle disparity, there can be quite a variation among individual fish with regard to muscle color, which may range from white through shades of pink and yellow

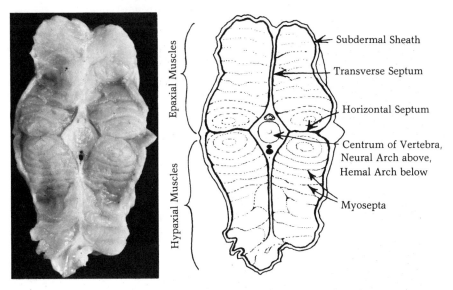

Figure 3.13. A cross section through the posterior body of a trout. (Photo by Steve Whitman.)

to a rich orange. Coloration is a result of plant pigments called carotenoids. Animals don't manufacture them, but herbivores get them from plants, and from there they are passed up through the food chain to the point where carnivores such as trout can pick them up. So the color of trout meat is a function of what fish — and their prey — have been eating. And although it's a commonly held notion that pink-meated trout taste better, carotenoids allegedly don't impart any taste to flesh; the preference must be a matter of the meat tasting better because it looks better.

In addition to the muscle associated with body contour and skeletal attachments, there is muscle involved with the workings of the internal organs. Its more notable tasks include moving blood through the vessels and food through the digestive tract.

The Digestive System

To get inside a trout without destroying internal organs, you may make an incision just in front of and to the left of the vent — the fish's left. Extend the cut forward (it will pass to the side of the left pelvic fin) as far as the pectoral girdle. Continue cutting upward along the back edge of the pectoral girdle, then backward along the upper part of the body cavity, and finally downward to the initial incision. The left body wall can now be lifted away (Figure 3.14). Trim away excess flesh from around the pectoral girdle, and when this is done cut the left pectoral fin off close to its base.

The body cavity and the organs within it are coated with a thin translucent membrane. In the roof of the cavity, along the midline, this membrane deflects away from the body wall and forms a double-

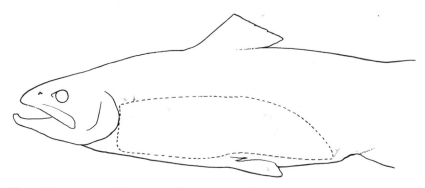

Figure 3.14. Portion of the body wall to be removed for viewing internal organs.

layered sheet which suspends the internal organs and holds them in place. Sandwiched between the two layers you can see blood vessels running out to the various organs.

The swim bladder is visible at the top of the body cavity on the far side of the membrane — its wall is whiteish, and in smaller fish the wall is rather translucent. This bladder is a hydrostatic organ that allows a trout to remain suspended in water at any depth. Flesh and bone are heavier than water, and without some buoyant structure they would sink; but when the bladder fills with air, buoyancy is gained. A fish in fresh water attains neutral bouyancy — a state in which the body will neither sink nor float upward — when the bladder occupies 7 to 10 percent of the body volume. In salt water, which is denser, the figure is around 5 percent. It's possible that the swim bladder also acts as a sound amplifier, making sound waves more audible to a fish.

In salmonids there's a narrow duct leading from the swim bladder to the esophagus through which air enters or exits from the bladder. One of the sounds made by trout (described as a "squawk") is thought to result from the rapid escape of air through this passageway. Probably the easiest way to locate the duct is to push some narrow, blunt instrument forward from the inside of the swim bladder (Figure 3.15).

Anything eaten by a trout passes through the mouth and back toward the esophagus, a short, muscular tube leading to the stomach. Water that enters along with food follows the same route taken by water during respiration, flowing into the gill chambers and out of the gill openings. Solid food enters the esophagus. Mucus produced by glands in the mouth lubricates the food, but no digestion takes place in the mouth because digestive enzymes are totally lacking in the mucus. The tongue is without muscles, but it does have taste buds, so something of the chemical nature of food can be perceived by the fish. Trout probably test foods on the basis of taste before swallowing, because items entering the mouth are sometimes quickly ejected.

A circular muscle at the junction of the esophagus and the stomach acts as a valve controlling the entry of food items into the stomach. Salmonids and other fish characteristically found in fresh water have a problem with water diffusing into their bodies, because their body fluids are saltier than the surrounding water. That the strength of their muscular valves is generally greater than that of valves in strictly marine fish has been associated with their need to keep excess water out of their bodies.

The U-shaped stomach is muscular and quite distensible (Figure 3.16). Glands within its inner wall produce mucus and hydrochloric

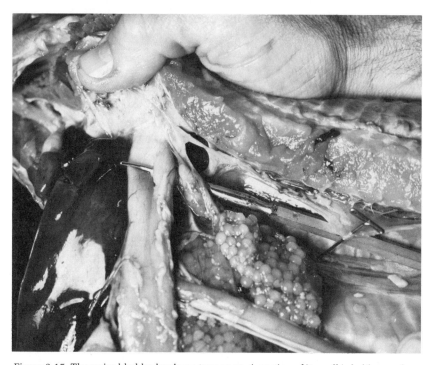

Figure 3.15. The swim bladder has been torn open. A portion of its wall is held away from the dorsal midline by a pin. The large metal probe is lying within the bladder. The narrow end of the probe has been pushed forward through the pneumatic duct and into the esophagus. The esophagus has been slit open so that the tip of the probe is visible. (Photo by Steve Whitman.)

acid, which are well mixed with food by the muscular action of the stomach. The acid medium inhibits bacterial decomposition.

The junction between the stomach and the intestine is marked by another muscular ring valve, which relaxes to allow the contents of the stomach into the intestine, a little bit at a time. In salmonids the first short portion of the intestine, the duodenum, is beset with a number of small, fingerlike pouches, the pyloric ceca. Because the construction of their walls is identical to that of the intestinal wall, some biologists think they might have evolved as a means of increasing the surface area of the digestive tract. There may be a lot of fat deposited around the pyloric ceca of well-fed trout, so that the ceca themselves are hidden from view.

The intestine extends toward the back of the body cavity. As food moves along the intestine, enzymes break it down chemically. Usable end products are assimilated into the bloodstream for distribution. Nondigestible matter continues on back to the rectum and is voided as feces at the anus.

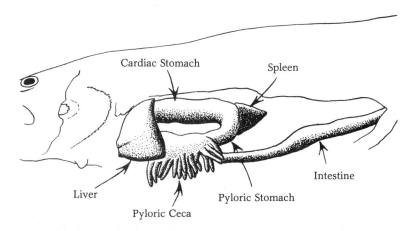

Figure 3.16. The digestive tract and other visceral organs. That portion of the U-shaped stomach lying closer to the heart is known as the cardiac stomach, while the portion that is closer to the pyloric ceca is called the pyloric stomach. (Photo by Steve Whitman.)

The size and color of the liver varies with the condition and nutritional state of a trout. One of the functions of the organ is the manufacture of bile, a greenish substance that emulsifies fat. Bile is stored in the gall bladder, a bubblelike sac on the upper part of the liver. Food passing from the stomach into the duodenum stimulates a flow of bile from the gall bladder into the duodenum by way of a duct that passes amongst the pyloric ceca. It appears that most digestion of fats in chinook salmon takes place in the ceca, and if this is so, the same is probably true for other salmonids as well.

The pancreas is a discrete, visible organ in many animals, but in trout it takes the form of little patches of glandular tissue in the membranes near the intestine. It's almost impossible to see. This pancreatic tissue produces digestive enzymes that make their way into the intestine by way of numerous fine, almost microscopic, ducts.

The spleen is located at the back end of the stomach, but it has no direct involvement with digestion. Rather, it acts as a storage site for blood, and some blood formation takes place in it.

The Reproductive System

The gonads — testes in males and ovaries in females — produce the sex cells. In both sexes they consist of a pair of longitudinal organs at the top of the body cavity on either side of the midline. Immature trout can be difficult to sex because their gonads are thin strips that don't look like much more than strands of connective tissue. But ovaries tend to have an orange hue, and if you look closely you might see they have a rather granular appearance. The little granules are developing eggs.

Ripe ovaries in mature females occupy a large space. But eggs are released from them well before spawning takes place, so the eggs are found free within the body cavity, virtually crowding some of the internal organs out of place. At the very back of the body cavity there is a passageway through which the eggs will pass during spawning; this leads to the genital opening on the urogenital papilla (Figure 3.17). When a ripe female trout is full of eggs you can strip them out of her by pressing on her belly and working your hand back toward the vent. It's a technique used for collecting eggs to be nurtured in hatcheries.

The testes in mature males (called "soft roes" in Great Britain) are flaccid white organs that sometimes have a faint pinkish cast to them (Figure 3.18). At the back of each there is a duct; the two ducts come together and lead to the opening on the urogenital papilla.

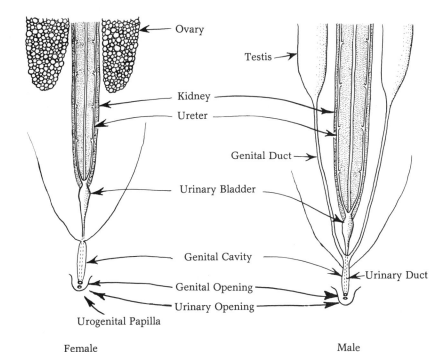

Figure 3.17. Male and female urogenital systems of salmonidae. (Modified from Henderson, 1967.)

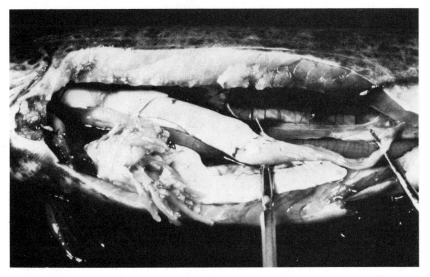

Figure 3.18. The reproductive system of a male brown trout ready to spawn. The more anterior of the two probes is beneath a testis. The other probe is supporting the genital duct. (Photo by Steve Whitman.)

The timing of reproductive activity in salmonids is controlled primarily by environmental factors such as light. Perception in these fish, of course, is through receptor organs (e.g., eyes), but when external factors are of a certain intensity, length, etc., they may also have an effect on the pituitary gland, a small organ at the base of the brain. The pituitary releases minute amounts of various hormones into the blood, and some of the hormones, once in general circulation, cause the reproductive organs to develop into spawning readiness. In short, the pituitary is the intermediary between environmental conditions and the actual physical changes associated with spawning in trout.

The gonads produce hormones too, and these, in addition to being involved with the production of sperm or eggs, are responsible for many features that distinguish males from females, such as color, fin development and general body and head form. Gonadal hormones also affect behavior; this will be covered in Chapter 7.

The Excretory System

The two kidneys, long organs visible through the membranous lining of the roof of the body cavity, are on either side of, and parallel to, the vertebral column. They filter wastes from the bloodstream and also function in blood formation. As a matter of fact, their dark red, almost red black color is a result largely of the blood-forming elements in them.

If you peel away the covering membrane you'll find the kidney tissue soft and easy to tease apart (Figure 3.19). And by working some of it away in the hind part of the kidneys, you can find the ureters — tubules that carry urinary waste out of the body. The ureters unite into a single tube that enters the urinary bladder, which in turn extends back and narrows to form a duct leading to the outside through an opening on the urogenital papilla. In both sexes the urinary opening is behind the reproductive opening.

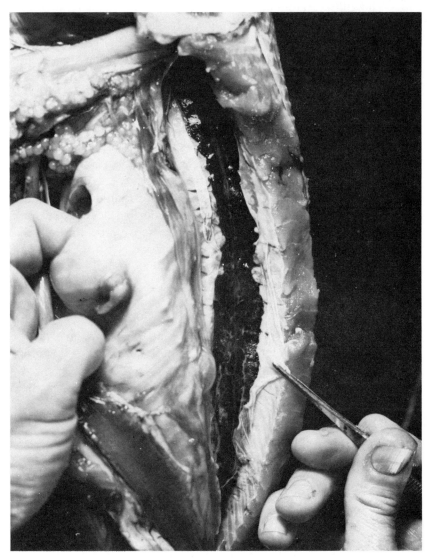

Figure 3.19. The swim bladder and some of the membranes which support internal organs have been deflected to show the kidneys. (Photo by Steve Whitman.)

The gills of salmonids function in excretion too. The huge total surface area represented by all those gill filaments and the constant wash of water through the gill chambers makes the gill area an excellent site for the voiding of unwanted substances. Some waste products are excreted in greater abundance by the gills than by the kidneys.

Blood and other body fluids of fish have a salinity of about 0.6 percent, which is higher than that of fresh water. This means that water will constantly diffuse into the bodies of freshwater fish, most of it through the thin, permeable tissues of the gills and mouth lining. Relatively little water enters through the skin, which has a scanty blood supply as well as a protective layer of mucus. In addition to the gain in water, there is a tendency for much-needed salts to be lost into surrounding water. The gain in water is compensated for by the fact that freshwater fish excrete copious amounts of very dilute urine, their total urine output being something like 10 times that of marine fish. In the kidneys, where urine is formed, there is some salt resorption, so that the salt loss is minimized. At the same time, some salt replacement is accomplished by the gills which, in addition to functioning in respiration and excretion, are specialized for the uptake of available salts in the water (even fresh water has traces). Salts are also picked up in food (Figure 3.20).

Marine fish have the opposite problem, since seawater is about 3.5 percent salt and there is a flow of water out of the body. To prevent dehydration, marine fish gulp large quantities of water. To handle the huge excess of salt entering the body, these fish have specialized cells in their gills that remove it from the bloodstream and excrete it into surrounding water. More salts are voided in feces.

Some species of fish can tolerate a broad range of salinities, but salmonids aren't necessarily among these. Hormonal changes associated with their migrations from salt to fresh water or from fresh to salt water must first bring about the physical changes necessary for coping with the new environment. Young Pacific salmon, for instance, can't make the transition to seawater until salt-excreting cells have developed in their gills. On the other hand, there are plenty of reports of trout in some coastal streams making daily excursions to salt water and back again. Perhaps in such cases the short stay in salt water — a matter of a few hours — isn't enough to stress the trout's system.

In Fresh Water

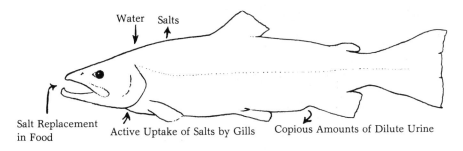

Water   Salts

Salt Replacement in Food   Active Uptake of Salts by Gills   Copious Amounts of Dilute Urine

In Salt Water

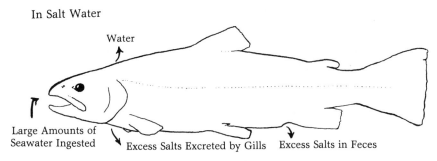

Water

Large Amounts of Seawater Ingested   Excess Salts Excreted by Gills   Excess Salts in Feces

Figure 3.20. Salt and water balance in fish resident in fresh water and salt water.

The Circulatory System

The basic features of the circulatory system include an extensive and intricate system of blood vessels, the blood within them, and a pump — the heart — to keep the blood in motion. It is this system that carries oxygen from the gills to tissues and wastes from all over the body to the organs of excretion. And it distributes nutrients and hormones.

The heart, composed almost entirely of muscle, lies quite a way forward in trout. Probably the best view of this organ can be had by placing a trout on its back and carving away, a bit at a time, the tissue of the isthmus, that extension of the body between the gill covers. In this way you'll ultimately gain entry into the cavity in which the heart is found.

The heart is a two-chambered pump. Blood returning through veins from all parts of the body — blood that has yielded up the bulk of its oxygen to the various tissues and simultaneously has taken on the waste products of metabolism — pours into the first of the two chambers (Figure 3.21). From there it is pumped to the second, more heavily muscled, chamber which is responsible for forcing the blood

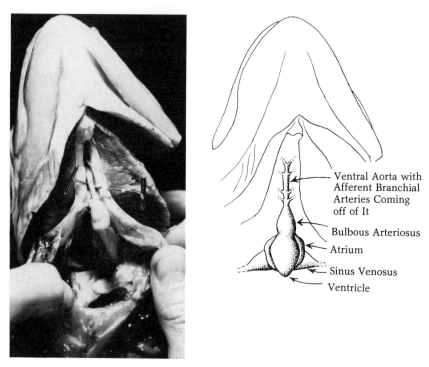

Ventral Aorta with
Afferent Branchial
Arteries Coming
off of It

Bulbous Arteriosus

Atrium

Sinus Venosus

Ventricle

Figure 3.21. A ventral view of the exposed heart of a trout. The afferent branchial arteries, which carry the unoxygenated blood to the gills, are not visible. Though the bulbous arteriosus and the ventricle are clearly seen in the photo, the atrium and the sinus venosus, both dorsal to the ventricle, are hidden in shadow. (Photo by Steve Whitman.)

out again into the arteries. Valves insure a flow in one direction only. When you consider the location of this delicate equipment, it's easy to see why small trout deeply hooked are seriously wounded.

In a reasonably good sized fish you can see a large vessel emerging from the front of the heart. Blood is pumped out through it and then up into the tiny capillary networks of the gill filaments, where oxygen diffuses into the blood and some wastes are expelled (Figure 3.22). Now freshly oxygenated, the blood is distributed throughout the body by a system of arteries. Immediately upon leaving the gills it flows up toward the roof of the mouth; from there some passes into the brain and other parts of the head, but most of it runs back through the body via a huge artery located just beneath the vertebral column. Here and there smaller arteries emanate from the big vessel to supply oxygenated blood to the muscle mass, the fins and various internal organs. Anyone seriously contemplating a dissection of the circulatory system usually injects it first with colored latex. After the latex solidifies, the vessels are located almost as easily as lines on a road map.

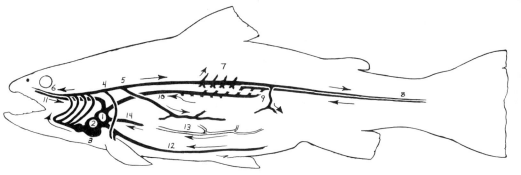

Figure 3.22. A diagrammatic depiction of the salmonid circulatory system. Oxygen-poor blood is returned from the body to the *sinus venosus* (1), a thin-walled reservoir from which blood is passed to the *atrium* (2), The atrium pumps blood to the *ventricle* (3), which then pumps it out to the *bulbous arteriosus,* the *ventral aorta,* and the *afferent branchial arteries.* In the gills oxygenation takes place. Freshly oxygenated blood then passes up into major arteries just dorsal to the mouth. Some blood runs anteriorly into the brain, eyes, etc., through the *carotid arteries* (6), but most runs posteriorly through the large *dorsal aorta.* At point 4 there emerge the *subclavian arteries* which supply the pectoral fins, and at point 5 the very large *coeliaco mesenteric artery* runs off the dorsal aorta and carries blood to much of the visceral mass. Its subdivisions carry blood to the liver, stomach, spleen, intestine, gonads, etc.

All along the dorsal aorta there are *segmental arteries* that carry blood to the body muscles and *renal arteries* that supply the kidneys. Some of these are shown at point 7. There is also a *posterior intestinal artery* (9) carrying blood to some of the more posterior viscera. By the time the dorsal aorta has reached the caudal region, it is known as the *caudal artery* (8).

All of the arteries feed microscopic capillaries, and it is there that oxygen and nutrients are yielded to the tissues and where wastes are brought into the blood. Capillaries then come together to form veins. All blood from the intestinal tract passes into the very large *hepatic portal vein* (13), which goes to the liver and breaks down into the microscopic spaces of that organ. This means that all assimilated food goes first to the liver.

The *caudal vein* carries blood forward from the tail region (8). It forms the *renal portal veins* which send branches to the kidneys (9). After filtration in the kidneys, blood passes into the large *posterior cardinal veins* (10), which return blood to the sinus venosus. The posterior cardinals also receive blood from segmental veins which drain the body musculature.

From elsewhere in the body, blood returns to the sinus venosus through *anterior cardinal veins* (11), which drain the head, *abdominal veins* (12), and *hepatic veins* (14) coming from the liver. Though it couldn't be shown on the diagram, most of this venous blood empties into short but voluminous *Ducts of Cuvier* just before passing into the sinus venosus. Incidentally, the diagram is a generalization and doesn't show the full complexity of the circulatory system. Only major flow patterns are included.

Each part of the body receives some arterial blood. Bigger arteries divide into smaller ones which, in turn, divide into beds of microscopic capillaries like those in the gills. From these, oxygen is at liberty to diffuse into the tissues, and wastes that have accumulated in the tissues make their way into the blood, from which they will later be removed by diffusion at the gills or perhaps by filtration at the kidneys. Blood passing through the capillary beds of the intestine receives nutrients that have been assimilated across the intestinal wall, and these are also distributed.

Just as the arteries have branched and branched again to yield the capillaries, the capillaries come together to form small veins which, like the feeder streams of a major river, contribute to the large veins carrying blood back to the heart. The total length of the circulatory system with its arteries, veins and capillary beds would amount to many miles, even in a foot-long trout.

The Nervous System

The most obvious parts of a trout's nervous system are the brain, housed within the skull, and the spinal cord, which emerges from the back of the brain and passes through the bony arches atop the vertebral column. Together the brain and spinal cord constitute the central nervous system. From this there arises a vast network of nerves which, like blood vessels, bifurcate many times; the terminal nerves are microscopic. Within the nerves are fibers that carry impulses to and from the central nervous system, which is responsible for the comprehension of incoming impulses and the proper direction of outgoing impulses. The whole is not unlike an electrical system.

The brain can be seen by skinning the top of the head behind the eyes and carefully breaking away the top of the skull. This would probably be more easily done on a small trout with its thinner bones. If you expose the brain without damaging it, some of its major regions will be fairly obvious (Figure 3.23).

In the front of the brain are the two olfactory lobes. These correspond to the huge cerebral hemispheres in man, the centers of learning, memory, reasoning, and the kind of intellectual activity we associate with our human mentality. But in trout virtually this entire region of the brain receives nerve fibers from the sensitive olfactory membranes and is therefore involved primarily with the perception of smell. In salmonids the sense of smell is at an amazingly high level of development and is a chief mechanism through which the fish receive impres-

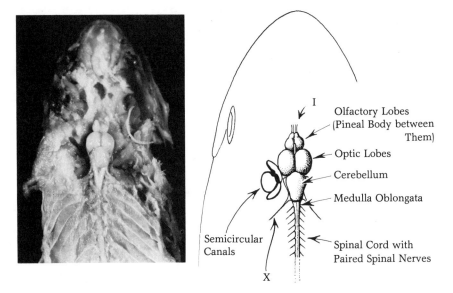

I
← Olfactory Lobes
(Pineal Body between
Them)

← Optic Lobes

— Cerebellum

— Medulla Oblongata

Semicircular
Canals

← Spinal Cord with
Paired Spinal Nerves

X

Figure 3.23. A dorsal view of the brain. Roman numerals indicate the first and last of the ten pairs of cranial nerves. The organ of audio-equilibrium is shown in black on the left side of the drawing. In the photo, one of the semicircular canals can be seen, which was removed and placed to one side of the brain. (Photo by Steve Whitman.)

sions from their environment. However, electrical stimulation of the olfactory lobes doesn't elicit any locomotor activity, and experimentalists who have surgically removed the lobes from fish report no changes in locomotion, vision, or balance. This indicates that the lobes are not involved with these activities.

In back of the olfactory lobes there are two large, bulbous optic lobes, perhaps the most noticeable region of the brain. Not only nerve fibers from the eyes, but also fibers from other receptors (e.g., taste buds and the lateral line system) lead to the optic lobes. There are also some nerve fibers in the lobes which control certain muscle activities; when these lobes are stimulated with electrodes, well-coordinated movements are generated in the muscles of the fins and eyes. It is also believed the optic lobes control much of a trout's behavior and learning, and if this is the case they function in much the same way as do our cerebral hemispheres.

Behind the optic lobes is the cerebellum, which coordinates muscular movements. It's normally the first part of the brain to be seen as one removes the top of the skull, because it represents the brain's uppermost extension. Behind the cerebellum, and partly covered by it, is the aftermost region of the brain, the medulla. This is basically a center for the control of vital processes — heart rate, respiration, and the like. The medulla tapers gradually into the spinal cord, which leaves the back of the skull through a large opening.

Some fibers of the outlying network of nerves are responsible solely for carrying impulses from sensory receptors, such as the taste buds or the eyes, into the central nervous system. These are sensory fibers, in contrast to the motor fibers which carry impulses from the central nervous system out to organs that respond to them — muscles, for example. The circuitry of the brain is exceedingly intricate, and an incoming impulse may be magnified so greatly that the resulting reaction is highly complex and quickly involves many parts of the body. An example is seen in the response of a trout that may have caught sight of a fleeting shadow, or one that has just felt the sting of a hook.

Sense organs are also part of the nervous system. They're designed to react to specific types of stimuli — light, pressure, certain chemicals, etc. — and to transform the stimuli into impulses that pass over sensory fibers to the central nervous system.

The sense of touch is well developed in trout, but our knowledge of a trout's receptors for heat and cold and for pain is scanty. As to the sense of taste, most studies in fish have been directed toward groups other than salmonids. In general, fish have demonstrated the ability to discriminate among the four qualities we know; sweet, sour, bitter, and salty. They appear to be especially sensitive to sweet and salty substances, detecting them in much lower concentrations than humans can. Rather than being restricted to the mouth, however, the taste buds of fish are found over many parts of the body, often being concentrated on the fins and in the tail area. Food introduced near the tail will often get a quick response.

The eye of a trout (Figure 3.24) is generally like a human eye, but there are some differences. In both, light passes through the pupil, a hole in the iris, and then through a clear lens which focuses upon the retina, the actual light-sensitive surface. The accommodation which allows images at varying distances to be brought into focus is carried out in humans by the changing shape of the lens, but in trout the lens is moved closer to or farther from the retina to achieve the same purpose. Humans can control the amount of light entering the eye by changing the diameter of the pupil, but in trout this doesn't take place, at least to any appreciable degree, so apparently trout can't accommodate to variations in brightness. As their pupils are of a rather large diameter, much of whatever light is in their surroundings is admitted to their eyes; this may be one reason that trout avoid brightly lit areas.

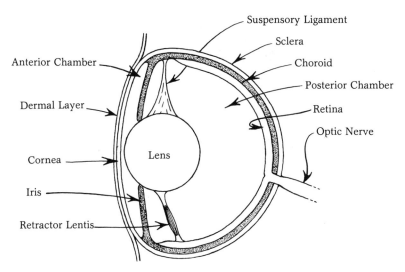

Figure 3.24. The trout eye: a diagrammatic depiction. (Modified from Parker and Haswell, 1963.)

On either side of the trout's head, at a level with the back of the brain, lie the mechanisms of the inner ear (Figure 3.25). These are involved both with hearing and with balance. On each side there are three semicircular canals and three other chambers, the latter containing little bits of bone known as the earbones or otoliths. The chambers in which the otoliths lie are lined with nerve endings. When a trout changes the orientation of its body, the otoliths, which aren't attached to anything, move about and hit nerve endings, thereby letting the trout know its position. If the fish goes over onto its right side, for instance, the otoliths bounce over to the right and hit the nerve endings on that side, creating impulses that lead to the awareness of being on the right side.

The sensation of motion arises largely from the semicircular canals — little fluid–filled hoops which, like the otolith-bearing chambers, are lined with fine nerve endings. When a trout moves, the fluids are set into motion and brush against the nerve endings. The semicircular canals, together with the otoliths and their associated nerve endings, convey information about angular accelerations; so as a trout turns, rolls, leaps and is buffeted about by currents, it is able to perceive both the motion and the orientation of its body at any moment.

Trout seem to hear quite well even though their ears lack external openings. It is probable that the area of the otolith-bearing chambers is responsible for sound reception.

Figure 3.25. Lateral (outer) view of the left organ of audio-equilibrium (inner ear). The blackened areas represent the three otoliths. (Modified from Parker and Haswell, 1963.)

The lateral line system in a salmonid consists of a mucus-filled canal located within the skin and running the length of the body. It communicates with the exterior via short canal branches that pass through holes in the lateral line scales (Figure 3.26). This system extends into the head, where it divides into several branches. The lateral line is sensitive to low frequency vibrations such as those generated by fish or other bodies moving through water. Pressure waves sent out by these bodies in motion are transmitted through the mucus of the system, causing hairlike nerve endings to vibrate. Trout may receive some information about currents through the lateral line. There's also a possibility that the system acts as a kind of sonar (echo-location) device by receiving back the reflections of waves initially sent out by the fish

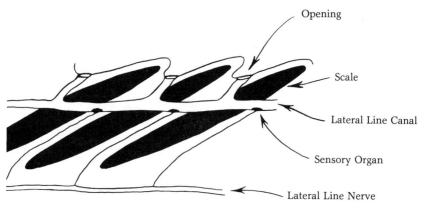

Figure 3.26. A diagrammatic representation of a portion of the lateral line system.

itself. Such a use certainly would aid navigation in waters where visibility is poor.

It's often implied that trout ''hear'' with the lateral line system in much the same way that we hear with our ears. But many biologists disagree and prefer to liken what is (probably) experienced by the fish with our sense of touch.

The Endocrine System

Organs that produce substances (hormones) released directly into the bloodstream are called endocrine glands. Even though the functions of the different hormones are so diverse that the various glands are not necessarily joined in a common purpose, the endocrines are considered together as the endocrine system. Gonads, the pituitary gland and the pancreas have already been mentioned. Some of the endocrines that are discrete, visible organs in the human body are scattered in trout, visible only under a microscope.

The systems of a trout body, functioning in unison in a healthy fish, make the total organism a smoothly operating unit. Around a bone framework a mass of contractile muscle tissue makes possible the movement of materials throughout the body as well as the movement of the body through water. Digestive, respiratory, and exretory systems are concerned with the entry of materials involved with energy metabolism, tissue replacement and growth, and with the outflow of waste products. The transport of materials to and from the tissues is accomplished by a circulatory system using a fluid medium, the blood. And a nervous system coordinates the operations of the other systems, receives and sorts stimuli from outside the body and is involved with the integration of appropriate responses to environmental situations.

4.

The Larger Parasites of Salmonids

> The difference between a carnivore and a parasite is simply the difference between living upon capital and income, between the burglar and the blackmailer.　　　　　　　　　—CHARLES ELTON, 1935

Anglers sometimes run across parasites in their trout. And were they to look a little harder they'd find a lot more, because parasites occur in virtually all wild populations. The organs and tissues of bodies offer potential habitats, and a variety of organisms have evolved the ability to make use of them, even though the chemical "climates" in bodies differ radically from those of the world outside. Any creature killed afield probably harbors a diversity of parasitic species, and the number of parasites in a single host may run into the thousands. This suggests that more parasitic individuals exist on the planet than free-living ones. In any case, it's a sure bet that trout parasites outnumber trout manyfold.

Trout parasites can be divided arbitrarily into two categories. On the one hand, there are the microscopic forms — including protozoans (single-celled animals), bacteria, and viruses — that multiply rapidly, are usually found in high numbers, and which are responsible for most of the contagious diseases in trout. On the other hand, there are multicellular organisms, most of them wormlike and large enough to be seen by the naked eye.

Some contagious diseases are disastrous under hatchery conditions, where the crowding of the fish favors the transmission of disease and can lead to epidemics. And even though all hatchery diseases can be traced back to wild sources, contagious diseases are of concern primarily to hatcherymen. Attempts to treat diseases in wild populations generally aren't made. Diseased fish in nature usually go unnoticed unless there are mass mortalities, since ailing individuals are more easily taken by predators, and those succumbing to some disorder are quickly cleaned up by scavengers.

The larger, multicellular parasites are the ones most often seen by anglers. Although such parasites are normally perceived as degenerate, they are really highly specialized for survival in their respective hosts, and many have life-styles of astounding intricacy. Some parasites may thrive in a variety of hosts, while others are highly host-specific, being able to survive only in a single host species. Though some may cause disease symptoms, many do virtually nothing in the way of detectable damage, and the fattest, healthiest looking trout may very well carry a substantial parasite burden.

It would be interesting to know how many trout are thrown away by anglers in a year just because some organism has been seen on them or in their flesh or viscera. The figure would be frightening. In 1970, a resident biologist in Yellowstone National Park told me that in the average month of July about 25,000 cutthroat trout are found in the park's trash containers; how many more are tossed off into the woods is anybody's guess. As it happens, more than 90 percent of the legal cut-throats in Lake Yellowstone harbor tapeworm larvae in their flesh. For anybody familiar with those trout such news hardly comes as a sur-prise, but the point is that a large proportion of the fish winding up in the trash bins are discarded because the larvae, which are more ob-vious than most parasites, have been seen. They're no threat to humans, though. Nothing parasitic in trout is harmful if fish are proper-ly cooked.

Monogenetic Flukes

Monogenetic flukes are small worms that parasitize aquatic vertebrates, especially fish. Most commonly they're found externally, and being small and soft-bodied, they may appear at first glance to be small bits of mucus, especially when they're found on hosts well en-dowed with mucus secretions. Monogeneans are hermaphroditic; each individual possesses both male and female reproductive systems. Their most striking external feature is a well-developed attachment organ located at the back end of the body and equipped with hooks or suckers, or with both. The name monogenetic fluke refers to the relatively simple life cycle, in which only a single host is involved. Typically, the eggs produced by these flukes yield tiny larvae, which swim about until they locate suitable hosts. Then they grow into adult worms.

One of the most common species of monogenetic fluke to occur on salmonids is *Gyrodactylus elegans* (Figure 4.1), a little creature of

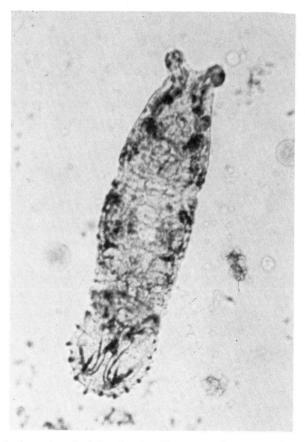

Figure 4.1. A speciment of *Gyrodactylus*. The two anchors, as well as the numerous marginal hooklets, are seen on the organ of attachment (the opisthaptor). (Courtesy of Doug Mitchum, Wyoming Game and Fish Department.)

perhaps a millimeter or two in length, with two large hooks and a battery of marginal hooklets on its attachment organ. Although these flukes show a special affinity for the tail and the dorsal fin, they might be found anywhere on a host's surface. Infested trout sometimes rub themselves on objects in an apparent attempt to rid themselves of the aggravation. When the fins are infested, their membranous portions may erode away, and heavy infestations might even kill a trout, especially if it's a small fish.

Gills are also a common site for infestation by monogeneans, such as the so-called trout gill worm (*Discocotyle salmonis*). These worms are close to a quarter of an inch long, showing up as yellow-white against the deep red of their host's gills. Here too, heavy infestations may do enough damage to cause the death of a trout.

Digenetic Flukes

Whereas monogeneans are pretty exclusively external parasites, the closely related digenetic flukes parasitize a wide variety of a trout's internal organs. The name digenetic refers to the fact that member species have relatively complex life cycles requiring two or more different hosts for completion. In such cases, the hosts harboring adult parasites are considered to be "final" hosts, while those in which larvae (the immature forms) are found are the "intermediate" hosts. The adult flukes are hermaphroditic, and species found in trout vary from about a twentieth of an inch to perhaps half an inch in length. Because many digenetic species infect the intestinal tract, the parasite eggs often pass from the host in feces; other possible routes to the outside include urinary and reproductive openings.

The life cycles of nearly all digenetic flukes conform to a general pattern, and *Crepidostomum cooperi* (Figure 4.2) is typical in this respect. It's a fairly common fluke found in the pyloric ceca of quite a few species of fish, including salmonids. Parasite eggs passing from trout (the final hosts) hatch in the water, liberating tiny, motile larvae that move about in search of suitable intermediate hosts. The general rule for digenetic flukes is that the first intermediate host is a mollusk — usually a snail, but sometimes a clam or a mussel. For this particular fluke, fingernail clams serve the purpose, and the hatched larvae penetrate them and undergo a number of physical changes, as well as an increase in numbers.

After a time, small, tailed fluke larvae emerge from the snail and swim away. The tailed larvae of some digenean species encyst on vegetation, dropping their tails and producing tough, protective coverings; in other species encystment takes place on (or in) second intermediate hosts. Either way, the encysted forms are infective to final hosts.

For *Crepidostomum cooperi*, mayfly nymphs serve as second intermediate hosts. The tailed larvae, recently emerged from a fingernail clam, penetrate the nymphs and encyst in their muscles. And when the infected nymphs metamorphose into adult mayflies, the encysted parasites survive and remain infective to trout. So if an infected mayfly, nymph or adult, is consumed by a trout, the immature parasites begin their development to the adult stage. Infection in the trout is therefore associated with the intake of food; this is frequently the case in parasitism.

Salmonids can serve as intermediate hosts for some fluke species.

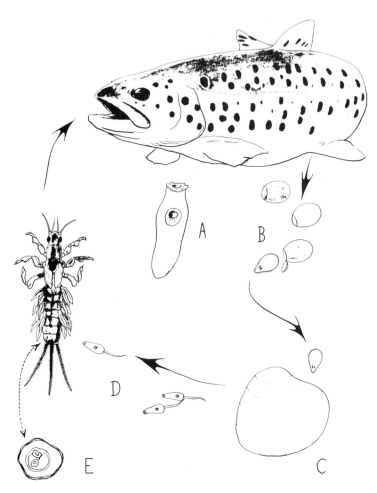

Figure 4.2. The life cycle of *Crepidostomum cooperi*. The adult worm (A) is located in thè pyloric ceca of the final host, in this case a brown trout. Eggs produced by such worms pass from the trout and hatch to yield miracidia (B), which enter fingernail clams (C). Within these first intermediate hosts the worms go through a number of larval stages, the last of which emerge as cercariae (D) and actively seek out mayfly nymphs. In the nymphs, the second intermediate hosts, cercariae encyst to become metacercariae (an example of which is shown isolated at E). If infected mayflies are eaten by trout, the metacercariae undergo development to adults. Various stages are shown in different degrees of enlargement.

In such cases, the encysted stage takes place in or on the fish. If encyst-ment is on the outside surface, it's common for pigment from the trout to be deposited around the cyst, thereby producing a black spot (Figure 4.3). In some areas of North America black spot is common, and heavi-ly infested fish given the impression of having been liberally sprinkled with coarse black pepper. Since encysted larval flukes are infective to final hosts, one would expect that the final hosts of flukes whose in-termediate hosts are trout would be creatures that eat fish. Ad so it is; one fluke species that causes black spot on trout reaches the adult stage in fish-eating birds such as herons and mergansers.

Tapeworms

Tapeworms are more difficult to generalize about than flukes, because within the tapeworm group there are various life cycle types and larval forms, and they don't all conform to a general pattern. On the other hand, they don't parasitize a wide variety of organs in their final hosts. With rare exceptions, they're found in the intestinal tract.

Most tapes are segmented. At one end there's a headlike struc-ture that may or may not have hooks and suckers. Behind the head is an unsegmented neck, and at the back of the neck the zone of segment pro-duction begins. As new segments are produced, older segments are

Figure 4.3. A trout (a preserved specimen) with an infestation of metacercariae, causing black spot. (Courtesy of Doug Mitchum, Wyoming Game and Fish Department.)

pushed toward the hind end, where they continue to develop. Like flukes, tapeworms are hermaphroditic, and each segment possesses complete sets of male and female reproductive organs. As any given segment is moved backward by new growth up front, it enlarges, its reproductive organs mature, fertilization occurs and eggs develop. Typically, then, the terminal segments are large and egg-filled. These detach from the worm body, and are passed out of the host with the feces.

Proteocephalus tumidocollus (Figure 4.4), a tapeworm that infests trout, belongs to that group of tapes most commonly found in freshwater fish. Mature, egg-producing worms of this species range in size from perhaps two or three inches up to about 16 inches, depending on the size of the trout and the number of worms present. The worms at first inhabit the trout's pyloric ceca, the blind pouches seen where the intestine joins the stomach. The ceca are too small to contain 16-inch tapes, but early worm development takes place there, and as growth continues the head end remains within a cecum while the body lengthens and grows out into the intestine proper. Egg-filled segments that have detached from the worm pass from the fish into the water, swell and burst, releasing multitudes of microscopic eggs that are infective to intermediate hosts. And intermediate hosts for this tapeworm are those little aquatic crustaceans called copepods. So copepods become infected by eating the tapeworm eggs, and within the copepods the larval stages develop which are infective to trout. When copepods are taken as food, as they often are by young trout, the larvae migrate to the pyloric ceca to begin development into adult tapes.

It's also possible for big trout to become infected if they feed on small trout that have eaten tapeworm larvae two to four weeks earlier. In other words, developing tapeworms can survive the process of being digested free of the body of the smaller fish and can then become established in the larger fish. This would explain new infections of this particular tapeworm in trout so large that they wouldn't normally be using copepods as food.

Trout may also serve as intermediate hosts for some tapes like *Diphyllobothrium cordiceps,* the parasite mentioned earlier in connection with Lake Yellowstone cutthoats. In this case, the larvae that are infective to final hosts (gulls and pelicans) are elongated, unsegmented creatures about a half an inch long that inhabit various tissues of the trout body. For the most part, tapes in trout, whether larval or adult, don't impair their host's ability to function unless they are present in

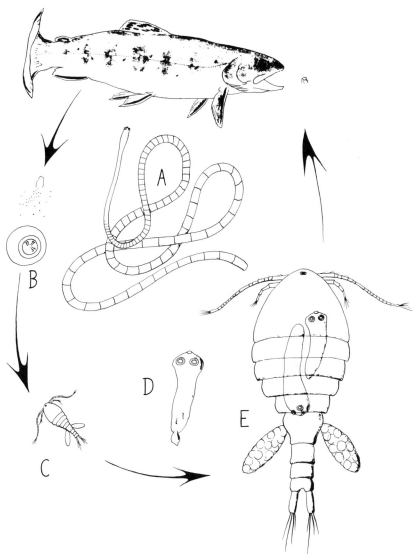

Figure 4.4. The life cycle of *Proteocephalus tumidocollus*. Adult tapeworms (A) are found in the digestive tract of the trout, the final host. Eggs which pass into the water, and which contain hexacanth larvae (B), are eaten by copepods (C), which are the intermediate hosts for the parasite. Within the copepods each hexacanth develops into a procercoid larva (an isolated example is shown at D). Procercoids grow and lose their taillike appendages to become plerocercoids (two of which are shown within a copepod at E). If copepods containing either procercoids or plerocercoids are eaten by trout, the larvae may develop to adult tapeworms. Stages and hosts are shown in different degrees of enlargement.

unusually great numbers. But very heavy infections of larvae have been known to kill trout.

Nematodes (Roundworms)

Most people have probably seen parasitic roundworms at one time or another, since these worms are often passed by domestic animals such as dogs and cats. The roundworm body is really quite simple in its basic design: an elongated cylinder tapering at each end, with an outer cuticle that usually gives a smooth and almost plasticlike appearance. Parasitic species vary in size from the microscopic to a foot or more in length, with females being larger than males.

Females produce large numbers of eggs, and within each egg a tiny larva develops that possesses the basic roundworm contour. Typically, this larva hatches and makes the change to the next larval stage by shedding (molting) its cuticle. A total of four molts are undergone (there are therefore four larval stages) before the adult stage is reached.

The apparent simplicity of this basic life cycle pattern is deceiving, because nematodes as a group have been immensely successful and have been able to establish themselves in a variety of habitats. Among those parasitizing animals, some have life cycles that are direct (involving no intermediate hosts), while others require as many as three hosts for completion of their life cycles. Migrations through hosts can be extensive, and virtually any organ or tissue may be parasitized.

Philonema oncorhynchi (which takes its species name from *Oncorhynchus,* the generic name of Pacific salmons) is found in the body cavity of Pacific salmon as well as in rainbows and brook trout (Figure 4.5). Adult worms inhabit the body cavity, and parasitized fish develop connective tissue that binds the internal organs together; in severe cases, normal function of the organs may be impaired (Figure 4.6). Eggs of the parasite hatch within the female worm, so the first-stage larvae are "born alive." The larvae then escape the body of their host when it spawns, passing out along with eggs or milt. It's also possible for entire female worms to be voided in this way, and if this happens they burst, liberating up to half a million tiny larvae. In either case, the larvae, once free in the water, tend to remain suspended for several days until copepods — the intermediate hosts — eat them. Within the copepods the tiny parasites molt a couple of times, and the resulting third-stage larvae are infective to young salmonids, which become infected by feeding on copepods.

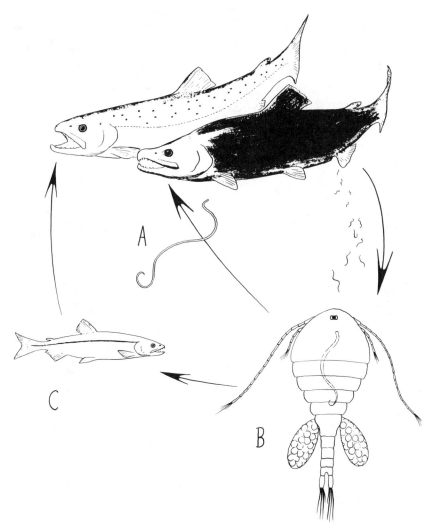

Figure 4.5. The life cycles of *Philonema oncorhynchi* and *P. agubernaculum* (see text). Adult worms (A) in the body cavity of salmonids bear their young alive. When passed into water the larval worms are eaten by copepods (B), in which development of the parasite occurs, resulting in a larval stage infective to the next host. Young salmonids may become infected with *P. oncorhynchi* by eating copepods harboring the larvae, as shown by the arrow leading from the copepod to the Sockeye salmon (in the foreground). With *P. agubernaculum,* an additional host is utilized, though whether or not it is always necessary is subject to debate. In this case, copepods are eaten by smelt (C). Salmonids, in turn, become parasitized by feeding on the smelt. Different degrees of enlargement were used for this figure.

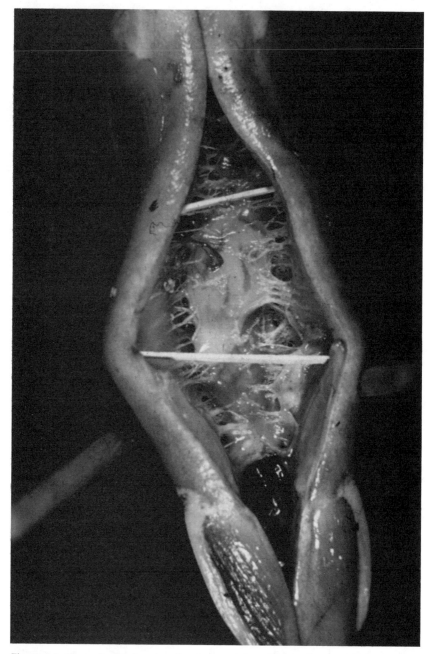

Figure 4.6. Visceral adhesions in a brook trout infected with *Philonema agubernaculum*. (Photo by Marvin C. Meyer, University of Maine. Printed through the courtesy of Glenn Hoffman, Fish Farming Experimental Station, U.S. Fish and Wildlife Service, Stuttgart, Arkansas.)

Sockeye salmon, in which the life cycle for this parasite was experimentally worked out, have themselves a four-year life cycle and die after spawning. As the fish journey to their freshwater spawning areas their sex organs develop, as do the sex organs of resident specimens of *Philonema oncorhynchi*. So it's probable that the life cycle of this worm is linked to development and hormonal change within the fish host. This isn't uncommon among parasites.

Another species of the same genus, *Philonema agubernaculum*, appears to have an interesting variation in its life cycle. In Maine, where the parasite is found in brookies and landlocked salmon, researchers were not able to establish infections in fish by feeding them infected copepods. But larval stages of the parasite were found in smelt which, in Maine, represent a major part of the diet of landlocks (see Figure 4.5). Larvae recovered from smelt were fed to trout and subsequently developed into adult worms, but whether the second intermediate host is necessary for completion of the life cycle hasn't been determined. Nor has the occurrence of a second intermediate host been demonstrated in the life cycle of *Philonema oncorhynchi*. Quite a few species of roundworms parasitize salmonids, and they can be found in diverse locations in the body. And, as they do for some tapeworms and flukes, trout occasionally serve as intermediate hosts in roundworm life cycles by harboring larvae infective to some fish-eating final host.

Thorny-headed Worms

These creatures are found as adults somewhere in the intestinal tract of their hosts, where they exist attached to the intestinal wall. Attachment is accomplished by the worm's most distinctive feature (the feature for which the worms were named), a proboscis that may either be everted from or withdrawn into a receptacle. The proboscis is armed with spines that generally project backward, so when it's embedded within the wall of the intestine the worm is firmly anchored. And because the proboscis can be lodged quite deeply within tissue, a heavy infection of thorny-headed worms can mean a badly damaged gut. These parasites are usually under an inch in length, and females are larger than males.

There's a uniform life cycle pattern in this group, and *Leptorhynchoides thecatus*, a thorny-headed worm found in a wide array of fish including salmonids, is typical (Figure 4.7). Larger females may reach an inch in length, while males are about half that size. Eggs produced by the female pass out of the fish host and into the water, where they're eaten by intermediate hosts. For thorny-headed worms that parasitize

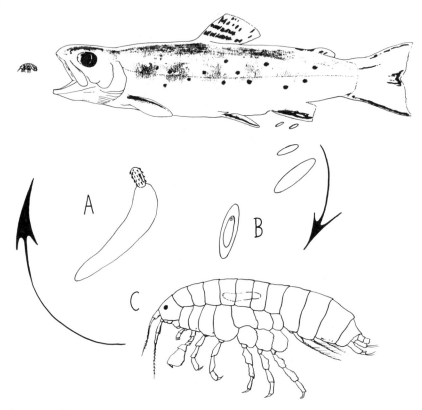

Figure 4.7. The life cycle of *Leptorhynchoides thecatus*. Adults (A) are located in the pyloric ceca of their final hosts. Eggs containing acanthor larvae are produced by the parasites and leave the host in the feces (B). If such eggs are consumed by amphipods (C), which serve as intermediate hosts, the acanthors develop into acanthella larvae. In the event an infected amphipod is eaten by a suitable trout host, the acanthellas develop into adult worms. Stages and hosts are shown in varying degrees of enlargement.

salmonids, some sort of small aquatic crustacean serves this role; in the case of *Leptorhynchoides*, the intermediate host is an amphipod. After about a month has elapsed, development of the parasite has led to the production of larvae that are infective to the final hosts. When trout feed on the infected amphipods, the parasites develop to the adult stage.

Glochidia

The females of freshwater clams retain developing larvae of their species in brood chambers until they're ready to be released. These larvae, called glochidia, are smaller than a period on a printed page, but despite their small size they are constructed much like adults. Looking at them through a microscope, you would be able to see two tiny shells with a muscle connecting them (Figure 4.8).

Fully developed glochidia are expelled from the parent clam in the current of water which passes continuously through adult clams. But in nearly all clam species, the glochidia have to spend a bit of time as parasites on fish if further development is to take place. Some species are highly specific in their choice of hosts, while others are less so. In any event, the glochidia must make contact with suitable species of fish hosts within days after leaving the parent, or they die. It's said that fish passing close to bottoms stir up sediments and glochidia, giving the latter an opportunity to make the necessary contact. If the gill filaments or fins of the fish are encountered, the tiny larval shells clamp shut on them. Host tissue may then grow around the larva so that a small, spherical, bubblelike cyst is formed. Even though a little bit of host tissue is consumed by the larva, no significant growth occurs. Instead, the larva's body is reorganized, resulting in an internal structure

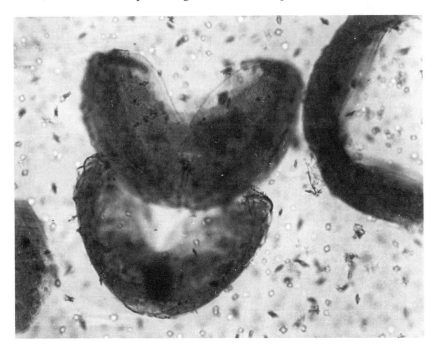

Figure 4.8. A microscopic view of glochidia larvae. The two specimens in the center are oriented so that their parted shells may be seen to best advantage. (Photo by Steve Whitman.)

similar to that of the adult. Periods of attachment to the host vary, but they usually last anywhere from a week to a month, after which the cysts slough off and the young clams continue development on their own.

By and large, glochidia do negligible damage unless they are found in unusually high numbers; in such cases gill damage may be sufficient to cause the death of a fish. Secondary infections on the fish by bacteria and fungi (i.e., the establishment of bacteria or fungi on any pre-existing wound or lesion) may occur too. Though salmonids are not hosts to glochidia as frequently as some other fish groups are, infestations among trout and salmon do occur.

Leeches

Less study has been devoted to leeches than to most of the parasitic groups, so not as much is known about the details of their life cycles. Some species are terrestrial and a few are marine, but most are freshwater, preferring shallow, slow-moving conditions. Leeches are most often thought of in connection with the practice of bloodsucking, and certainly most leeches can and do take blood meals from other animals, but some species are predatory, and a few others are scavengers. They tend to be subdued in color, with blacks, browns and olive greens being common. Some possess spots and lines in various patterns.

Leeches are closely related to earthworms and, like them, have segmented bodies. Many of the anatomical features of the parasitic leeches are associated with bloodsucking, and suckers at both ends of the animal aid in attachment to a host. The smaller of the two suckers is at the front of the body and generally has the mouth located within it. The mouth itself is equipped either with bladelike jaws for making incisions or with a long proboscis which can be forced into the host. Glands in the region of the mouth produce anticoagulants that keep blood flowing freely. The suckers also aid in locomotion, enabling a leach on a solid substrate to move along in inchworm fashion. When swimming, the body flattens and undulates vertically.

Some leeches attach to a host only for a blood meal, but species of the fish leech group remain attached for long periods, usually departing from the host only to mate. In general, the damage they inflict is in direct proportion to the number of leeches attached. Still, any time the external surface of a fish is damaged, even slightly, an invasion of the site by bacteria or fungus becomes a distinct possibility.

Leeches are hermaphroditic, and their mating act is a process of cross-fertilization in which the female system of each copulating individual gets sperm from another leech. Later, when eggs are deposited, a cocoon is secreted and receives the eggs. Cocoons are most commonly attached to vegetation or underwater objects, but sometimes are buried in mud or attached to hosts. Some species of leeches even retain their cocoons, attaching them to the lower surfaces of their own bodies. There are no intermediate hosts, nor are there any larval stages radically different in appearance from adults. Young individuals are similar to mature specimens, and are ready to attach to a host when they hatch.

Although some leech groups seem to prefer certain broad categories of hosts, they're not particular about the exact species of their hosts. Fish leeches, for instance, are seldom found on hosts other than fish, but they parasitize a broad array of fish species. The leeches most commonly reported on trout are several species of *Piscicola*, one of the fish leech genera (Figure 4.9).

Figure 4.9. *Piscicola* sp., removed from the exterior of a cutthroat. (Photo by Steve Whitman.)

Parasitic Copepods (Fish Lice)

Copepods have already been mentioned in connection with their roles as intermediate hosts in the life cycles of some of the worm parasites. As members of the same general animal groups as the crabs and crayfish, they have similar anatomical features, including external skeletons or shells, and jointed appendages. Most species are free-living and occupy important positions in aquatic food chains, but quite a few have taken up the parasitic existence. Those parasitizing fish are generally found on the surface of the body, on fins, gills, and in the mouth, where they procure nourishment from host tissues. And even though they aren't really related to lice, the term "fish louse" has long been applied to them.

Adult fish lice are often so bizarre in appearance that they bear little resemblance to free-living copepods or, for that matter, to anything else fairly familiar. In most fish lice, the mouthparts have become adapted for piercing and sucking in host tissues, and certain appendages have been modified into "holdfast" organs used for attachment. Like the leeches, parasitic copepods have received only spotty study, and most of what is known about their life cycles is based on observations of infected hosts rather than on experimental evidence. But their life cycles appear to be quite simple. The eggs are typically carried in sacs on the female body. With the egg-laden female still on the host fish, a tiny larva hatches from each egg. Thereafter a series of larval stages lead up to the adult form. Some larval forms characteristically attach to the host fish, while others swim freely in open water and are therefore able to find new hosts.

Perhaps the fish lice most often seen by trout fishermen are species of *Salmincola*. *Salmincola edwardsii* (Figure 4.10), for example, is a common external parasite of brook trout in eastern North America, and because it's so easily seen it sometimes generates complaints of "wormy" or "grubby" fish. This parasite is found in the mouth and gill areas and on fins, and though it's sometimes mentioned in textbooks as parasitizing brook trout only, there are occasional reports of its presence on other salmonids. Normally, only the female is seen, because while she is several millimeters long, the male is about half a millimeter in length — very nearly microscopic. The female attaches herself to a host fish by means of a saucerlike structure, which is embedded in the host's tissue and which serves as a mechanism for absorbing blood and tissue fluid. The parasite's mouthparts have evolved into elongated structures that attach to the saucerlike organ, so she

Figure 4.10. Brook trout with a heavy infestation of *Salmincola edwardsii*. (Department of Natural Resources-State of Michigan.)

Figure 4.11. *Salmincola* infesting a trout. (Department of Natural Resources-State of Michigan.)

looks like a tiny human clinging to the host with outstretched arms (Figure 4.11).

Another species of fish louse, *Lernaea cyprinacaea*, is apparently able to infect all freshwater fish, and can be found anywhere on the body, fins, or gills (Figure 4.12). Only the female of this species is parasitic as a fully developed adult. Her elongated body is up to an inch long and sports hornlike projections up front, and while on a host her entire head and neck, projections and all, are embedded in the host's tissue. As she feeds on blood and tissue fluid, she causes a lot of damage; a heavy infestation can kill a fish.

In genus *Argulus* (Figure 4.13) there are a number of species that can infest salmonids. Actually, *Argulus* isn't one of the true copepods, but it's sufficiently related for member species to go by the name of fish lice. These creatures are rather conspicuous: flat and disclike, they are usually from a quarter to three-quarters of an inch in length. Females are larger than males, but otherwise the sexes are pretty much alike in appearance.

Unlike other fish lice, *Argulus* doesn't stay permanently attached to its host. Adult parasites can move about on a fish and might even

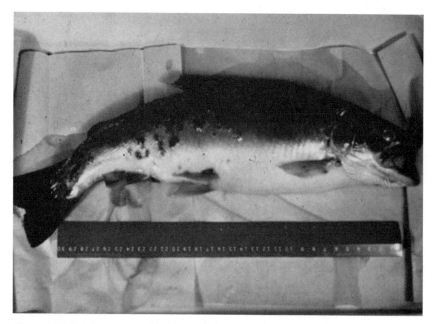

Figure 4.12. Rainbow trout with a heavy infestation of *Lernaea cyprinacaea*. (Department of Natural Resources-State of Michigan.)

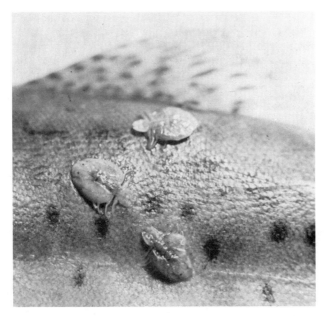

Figure 4.13. Specimens of *Argulus* on a host. (Courtesy of Doug Mitchum, Wyoming Department of Game and Fish.)

leave the host to swim about for short periods. When a blood meal is to be taken, they insert a sting into the host. Rather than carrying egg sacs, females deposit eggs in little gelatinous masses on stable objects in the water. The larval stages bear a resemblance to those of the true parasitic copepods.

As a group, the fish lice don't pose a threat to wild trout populations, possibly because they rarely occur in great numbers on any single fish. But in hatcheries, where potential hosts are so crowded, heavy infestations are found from time to time.

Lampreys

In North America there are 14 species of lampreys and of these, 6 are parasitic. The best known of them is the anadromous Atlantic sea lamprey, *Petromyzon marinus,* which became famous by invading the Great Lakes and raising havoc with trout fishing there. The Pacific Coast also has an anadromous sea lamprey, *Entosphenus tridentatus,* that ranges from California to Alaska. Other species are strictly freshwater. The life cycle pattern is similar for all species, but in the nonparasitic lampreys the adults don't feed and so never grow larger than the ammocoetes from which they metamorphose.

There was a time when lake trout were the mainstay of the commercial fishing catch in much of the Great Lakes region. Anglers benefited too, and older sportsmen still reminisce about fabulous catches. All during the 1930s the Great Lakes were yielding 10 million pounds or more of trout annually, and the local economies of lakeside towns like Charlevoix, Michigan, and Port Washington, Wisconsin, rested largely on the abundance of the big lakers.

But even as the trout fishery was thriving, its ruin — in the form of the Atlantic sea lamprey, *Petromyzon marinus* — was making its way inland from the Atlantic Ocean, passing through canals that had been constructed as aids for shipping. Niagara Falls had historically posed a barrier to the entry of ocean fish into the upper Great Lakes, but that ended with the completion of the Welland Canal in 1829. At first the sea lampreys fared badly, because Lake Erie waters were too warm and its spawning areas poor, and it wasn't until the 1920s that specimens were found in the lake. By the 1930s lampreys had become established in Lakes Huron and Michigan, where conditions were suitable for their species, and just after World War II they were found in Lake Superior.

Lake trout were excellent hosts for lampreys, since like the lampreys they are residents of deep water. The resulting parasitism caused trout populations to plummet. By 1960, the total trout catch for Lakes Michigan and Huron combined wasn't quite 2,000 pounds, and the take in Lake Superior was almost as bad. Once prosperous fishing towns were turned into centers of economic depression.

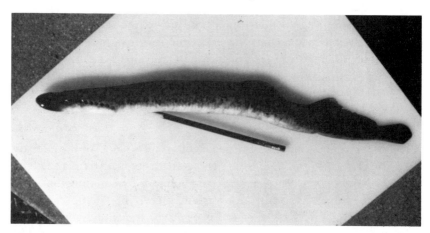

Figure 4.14. An adult lamprey. (Courtesy of Russell Daly, Wisconsin Department of Natural Resources.)

A good-sized lamprey can attain a length of nearly three feet (Figure 4.14). Perhaps the most prominent adult feature is the cuplike mouth beset with numerous hard projections (Figure 4.15). With this the lamprey can attach itself to virtually any external part of a fish host, causing considerable damage in the process. The tongue is armed too and is rotated back and forth as a rasp, so that a deep wound is produced on the host. Salivary secretions chemically break down the tissues of the host and keep blood flowing freely (Figure 4.16).

Like many of the salmonids, the Atlantic sea lamprey is anadromous, and though basically marine in the adult stage it has been immensely successful in adapting to fresh water. In late winter in the Great Lakes, adults congregate at the mouths of tributaries to begin their upstream migration, during which large numbers of them may be seen in particularly shallow and difficult waters, floundering clumsily as if doing a parody of a salmon run. A lamprey migration can last on into spring.

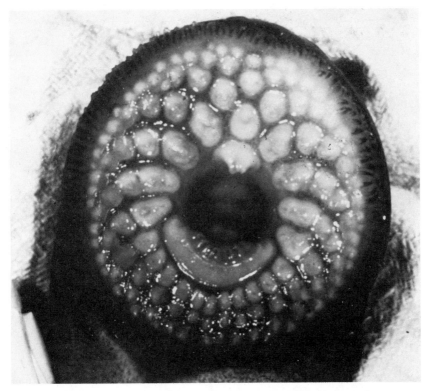

Figure 4.15. The mouth of a lamprey. (Courtesy of Russell Daly, Wisconsin Department of Natural Resources.)

Figure 4.16. A rainbow exhibiting a wound left by a feeding lamprey. (Courtesy of Russell Daly, Wisconsin Department of Natural Resources.)

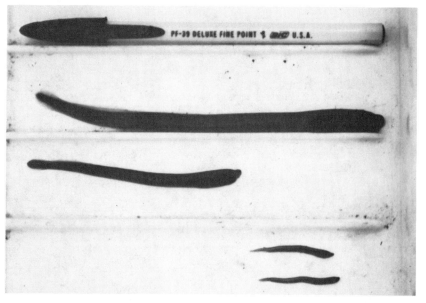

Figure 4.17. *Ammocoete* larvae of various sizes. (Courtesy of Russell Daly, Wisconsin Department of Natural Resources.)

Lampreys spawn in moderately swift runs, dying a matter of hours thereafter. In two or three weeks, the eggs hatch to yield the larval stage of the lamprey, the ammocoete (Figure 4.17). Superficially, these little creatures resemble adults, being elongated and jawless, but their feeding mechanism allows only for the filtering of organic material from the water. Just a quarter of an inch long at hatching, they remain in the nest for about three weeks before drifting downstream into quieter waters, where they burrow into soft bottom deposits to spend the rest of their larval lives. After four to six years, at which time they're about six inches long, they undergo the metamorphosis that yields adult features, and then migrate downstream to the lake to begin their parasitic existence. When feeding, adults remain attached to the host until sated, or until the host succumbs; at times they remain on the same fish for weeks on end. Lampreys remain in a lake from 12 to 20 months before embarking on their spawning run.

A variety of measures have been used to control the sea lamprey in the Great Lakes, including electric weirs in spawning tributaries and poisons that act selectively against the ammocoete larvae. So even though the battle against this disastrous introduction is by no means over, the lamprey isn't quite the immediate threat that it was a few decades ago.

Fungi

Fungi are plants which, lacking chlorophyll, are unable to manufacture their own food. Instead, they use as sources of nutrition organic substances of plant or animal origin, and a number of species parasitize living tissue.

Most anglers are aware of the fact that fish occasionally fall prey to fungus infections, and many have seen the fine, cottony fuzz that covers the bodies and fins of infected fish, projecting perhaps a quarter of an inch beyond the flesh. The fungus species responsible for the vast majority of infections in fish, and in fish eggs too, is *Saprolegnia parasitica* (Figure 4.18). It's common in fresh waters all over North America, and it thrives in all seasons. It can infect a wide variety of plant and animal tissues, living or dead, and good growths can often be obtained by placing a bit of meat into some pond or streamwater.

The growing fungus parasite is composed of branching, threadlike hyphae, and the entire mass of hyphae taken collectively is called a mycelium (Figure 4.19). Though basically whitish in color, this

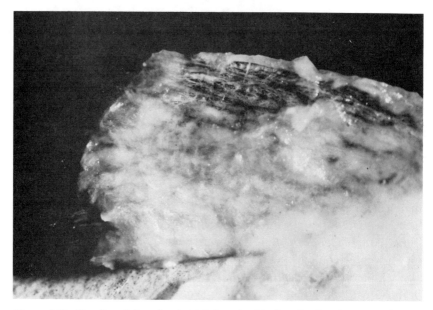

Figure 4.18. The dorsal fin of a trout infected with *Saprolegnia*. (Courtesy of Doug Mitchum, Wyoming Game and Fish Department.)

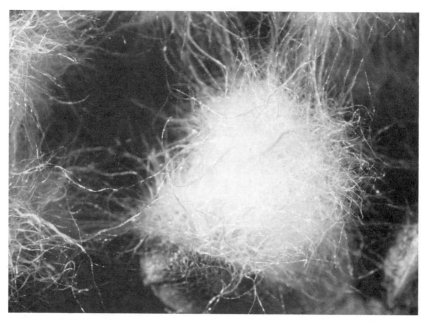

Figure 4.19. An enlargement of the mycelium of *Saprolegnia parasitica*. (Courtesy Carolina Biological Supply Company.)

mass often traps debris and takes on a dirty appearance. Some of the hyphae form a rootlike network that anchors the mycelium in the food source and carries on the processes of digestion and absorption. Hyphae extending beyond the tissue — and making up the visible part of the mycelium — possess reproductive bodies on their tips.

Reproduction normally takes place through the manufacture of spores, which develop in clublike structures on the tips of the exposed hyphae (Figure 4.20). When fully developed, spores escape into the water, where they are free to establish infections elsewhere. When a spore comes to rest on a suitable host surface it begins to produce a hypha, and a new mycelium is thereby begun. On occasion other kinds of spores are produced, and even less frequently sexual reproduction takes place, with male and female reproductive organs forming on the tips of hyphae. Fertilized eggs form resistant coverings and undergo a period of rest; when they germinate, hyphae are produced.

It's believed by many authorities that in order for *Saprolegnia* to become established on living fish, it must have access to a pre-existing wound or an infected area or to tissue weakened in some way. But once established, mycelia spread to the extent that they envelop the host fish and kill it. Fish appear to be especially vulnerable to infection when in a weakened condition, which often occurs in the wake of spawning activity. In fish eggs, infections begin in dead eggs rather than live ones,

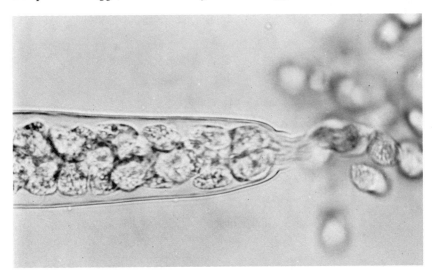

Figure 4.20. A microscopic view of spores of *Saprolegnia parasitica* being released. (Courtesy Carolina Biological Supply Company.)

but once an infection gets started the healthy eggs in a mass also become enveloped and are killed.

The parasites mentioned in this chapter are only examples of the groups they represent; there are hundreds of species that use salmonids as hosts. And salmonids may serve as intermediate hosts for three different parasites that infect man. People become infected by eating parasite larvae along with raw or improperly cooked fish. Two of these parasites are digenetic flukes, but they aren't found on the North American continent, at least not yet. The third, the so-called broad fish tapeworm, is indigenous to North America and is frequently found in cultural groups in which fish is eaten essentially raw. This giant tapeworm can exceed a length of 20 feet. But none of this should dampen an angler's enthusiasm, because cooking kills parasites and therefore renders them harmless.

There is an aesthetic side to parasitism, just as there is to all of biology. You've got to marvel at the seemingly insurmountable odds that some of these creatures overcome in completing their complex life cycles. Parasitism, like predation, is intimately woven into the fabric of life in the wild. And it's quite as legitimate as any other mode of existence.

5.

The Aquatic Medium

And now for the water, the element that I trade in. The water is the eldest daughter of the creation. . . .　　　　　—Izaac Walton, 1676

To a large extent the physical and behavioral traits of salmonids have been determined by the medium in which they spend their lives — its density and viscosity, its transparency, its ability to carry dissolved substances and the like. Take viscosity, the resistance a medium offers to bodies trying to move within it: it is about a hundred times greater for water than it is for air, so mobile aquatic creatures have tended to evolve streamlined proportions and relatively friction-free surfaces that allow them to slip through their medium with a minimum of resistance.

The great density of water (hundreds of times more dense than air) gives tremendous buoyancy to submerged bodies, making it possible for aquatic creatures to expend less energy than terrestrial forms to support their bulk. But since a trout's tissues, taken collectively, are denser still than water, a fish would tend to sink — rather slowly — were it not for the swim bladder. By gulping air and forcing it into this bladder, a trout can achieve a condition of neutral buoyancy, so that rather than rising or sinking it literally hangs in one spot. And when swimming hurriedly into deeper water, a fish may suddenly expel air from the bladder to increase the density in its body and so hasten its descent.

All animal life depends on plants, and even though salmonids don't consume vegetation as a rule, the creatures they eat may be plant feeders or may themselves eat plant feeders. In water as on land, the base of the food chain consists of plants that manufacture food by using light as an energy source. Anything that prevents light from penetrating into water shuts off the energy supply for the entire aquatic community. This happens when an excessive amount of silt clouds the water or when snow cover prevents light from penetrating lake ice.

Some of the light falling on water will be reflected away from the surface. Rays that do enter the water, because they're entering a denser

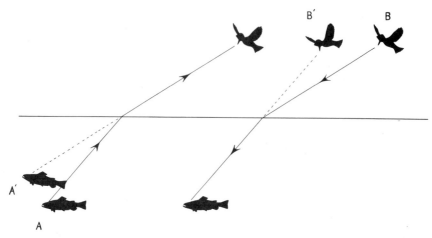

Figure 5.1. Because of refraction a subsurface object at A will appear to be at A' to an observer above the surface. This effect will be greater at the head of the trout shown in the figure because, being farther from the observer, light coming from it will be bent to a greater degree. The entire fish therefore appears somewhat tilted and a bit magnified. Likewise, an object above the surface at B will appear to an observer beneath the surface to be at B'.

medium, are bent (refracted) to become more vertical (Figure 5.1). Light rays reflected off of an underwater object and up toward the eye of an observer above the surface are also refracted, but when they enter the air — the less dense medium — they are bent to become less vertical. So things under water are not right where they appear to be to above-water viewers, and as the opposite is true as well, an object above water will not be exactly where a trout perceives it to be. In order to vault out of the water and nab a flying insect, or to navigate by the sun, both of which they're clearly able to do, trout have to be able to compensate for the angle of refraction.

Most trout fishermen, it seems, are very much aware of the trout's "window," that conical field of view with a 97° angle within which the trout's above-water vision is confined (Figure 5.2). Some anglers will literally crawl to the water's edge, apparently under the impression that if they're outside the cone they'll be totally concealed from the trout's view. But refraction allows some light from nearly all points above the surface to be brought into the trout's window, so trout can detect objects close to the surface for a considerable distance. Of course, a rough water surface does a lot to conceal objects from a fish. The window, incidentally, isn't due to anything unique about the salmonid eye; it's a result of a characteristic of water.

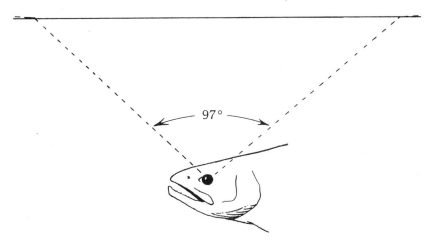

Figure 5.2. The window of a trout is that portion of the surface through which light rays from above are visible. Its diameter varies with the depth of the trout (the closer to the surface the fish is, the smaller the diameter), since the angle of the cone of vision is always 97°.

Water has another unusual characteristic; of all the earth's natural substances, water has the greatest ability to absorb or to give off heat while itself undergoing relatively little change in temperature. The wild temperature fluctuations that can occur above the surface aren't felt nearly as profoundly within a body of water, and aquatic creatures enjoy relative temperature stability.

Dissolved Solids

All natural waters contain hosts of dissolved substances. Which ones are to be found in solution in any given body of water depends primarily on the nature of the ground over which the water flowed or through which it percolated, so there's a lot of variation among waters of different areas. The values in Table 5.1 are averages for waters from different locations and surely would encompass most trout waters in North America.

Many of these substances are important to aquatic life. Plants use magnesium in the manufacture of chlorophyll; microscopic algae called diatoms use silicon in making their delicate and uniquely beautiful shells; calcium is used as shell material by mollusks, and acts to render heavy metals less toxic to fish — an example of how some substances have a bearing on the effects of other substances.

Table 5.1. Values in milligrams per liter for some dissolved solids in some American rivers. Most trout streams would fall within the ranges shown.

Dissolved Solid	Range (mg/1)
Bicarbonate	40 — 180
Sulfate	11 — 90
Chloride	3 — 170
Calcium	15 — 52
Magnesium	3.5 — 14
Sodium and potassium	6 — 85
Total dissolved solids	72 — 400

SOURCE: Based on Hart et al., 1924, as printed in Warren, 1971.

Perhaps the most notable of the dissolved substances in water are the phosphates and nitrates. Both are indispensable for plant growth, and because all aquatic animals ultimately depend upon plant production, insufficiencies in either limit biological productivity. In most lakes and in some rivers the phosphate level constitutes the single factor that limits the aquatic community as a whole.

An excellent demonstration of how a dissolved substance can affect an aquatic community and the trout within it was made in Oregon by Charles Warren and his colleagues. To a small trout stream they added a continuous flow of sucrose, a nutrient utilized by bacteria found in the stream. The added sucrose favored growth of the bacteria which, in turn, were fed upon by herbivorous insects, especially midges. The increased numbers of midge larvae were consumed by carnivorous insects, notably stoneflies and dobsonflies, whose numbers also went up. And with the increased insect supply there was a rise in the production of cutthroat trout within the stream.

Although the addition of nutrients to water causes an increase in productivity, the ultimate result may not be favorable to salmonids. An increasing abundance of nutrients — a process known as eutrophication — leads to increases in organic material, and the decomposition of this new volume of material makes increased demands on available oxygen and favors the accumulation of sediments. Over time, then, a lake tends to fill in, aging as it were, until it eventually becomes a shallow, heavily vegetated eutrophic lake not ideally suited to the needs of trout.

Eutrophication is a natural process, but certain activities of man can speed it up, and in some areas have now become its chief causes. Agricultural runoff and raw sewage add tremendous quantities of nutrients to waterways, with predictable results. Explosive increases in plant growth resulting from phosphate detergents alone are sometimes newsworthy. This particular consequence of human activity has been referred to as "cultural eutrophication," and many a trout lake has deteriorated because of it. In typically fast-flowing trout streams, high nutrient levels aren't nearly as critical since the physical agitation of the water inhibits excessive plant growth.

Dissolved Gases

Both oxygen and carbon dioxide are found dissolved in trout waters, and both are essential to aquatic communities. Oxygen, of course, is needed for respiration in both plants and animals, a process in which carbon dioxide is given off as a waste product. On the other hand, carbon dioxide is required by plants in their manufacture of food via photosynthesis, and in this case oxygen is given off. The presence of these gases, therefore, hinges largely upon resident aquatic life — on the respiration and photosynthesis taking place. If a particular body of water is especially rich in plant life, profound fluctuations in the concentrations of both gases may take place over a 24-hour period, because photosynthesis ceases at night while respiration continues around the clock.

Dissolved oxygen is found in water in concentrations of up to about 30 parts per million. If the quantity of oxygen is too low, the activities of fish become restricted; at even lower levels fish die. It is difficult, and even misleading, to give a definite minimal level of oxygen deficiency which can be tolerated by a given species of fish, because time is a critical factor in asphyxiation. A brook trout, for example, might tolerate a certain low level of oxygen for an hour or two, but succumb in twelve or twenty-four or forty-eight hours. In general, though, salmonids require a highly oxygenated environment, and a minimum acceptable level of dissolved oxygen for trout water would be in the neighborhood of four parts per million.

Aquatic biologists often refer to "B.O.D.," which stands for "biological oxygen demand." It's a measure of the oxygen required in a given mass of water to allow for the decomposition of organic material by oxygen-requiring microorganisms. As the amount of organic debris to be decomposed accumulates, B.O.D. — the demand for oxygen — goes up. By and large, a high B.O.D. doesn't bode well for salmonids, with their need for highly oxygenated water. In badly polluted waters the B.O.D. may be so high that the oxygen is virtually used up in the process of decomposition, leaving little or none for the normal respiratory processes of aquatic organisms. The physical agitation of water, however, which occurs when water is blown by the wind or tumbling over rocks in a stream bed, allows for aeration and the replenishment of dissolved oxygen.

In most fresh waters, the dissolved carbon dioxide level ranges from 0 to around 20 parts per million. It derives primarily from the atmosphere and from the respiration of aquatic organisms. A very high rate of decomposition, in addition to lowering oxygen levels, can raise the carbon dioxide level to as high as 50 parts per million. When there's a major rise in carbon dioxide, vertebrates ventilate more rapidly; in the case of trout, one would see the opercula operating at an increased rate. At extremely high levels the gas becomes toxic. Salmonids aren't adversely affected by the concentrations normally seen in nature, but high doses have an anaesthetic effect on them, and concentrations of up to 600 parts per million have been used to make them easier to handle. It's a dangerous practice, though, because prolonged exposure is lethal.

Nitrogen makes up about 80 percent of the atmosphere, but as it isn't easily soluble it's normally found only in low concentrations in water. However, as one goes deeper in water, pressure becomes greater because of the accumulating weight of water above; and as pressure increases so does water's ability to dissolve gases. (Also, cold water dissolves more gas than warm water can.) Water passing through dams is sometimes subjected to high pressures, so that increased amounts of nitrogen are dissolved into the water from air bubbles. Fish lying in deep pools below dams may find themselves in water that is highly saturated with dissolved nitrogen, and on such occasions their body fluids will also take on high concentrations of the gas. If these fish then swim rapidly into shallower water, the sudden decrease in pressure causes some nitrogen to come out of solution, and bubbles begin to appear in their tissues. Aptly called nitrogen bubble disease, this fatal disorder is precisely the same as the bends that affect divers who ascend too rapidly after having been in deep water for prolonged periods. In the Pacific Northwest, where there are a lot of anadromous salmonids and plenty of dams to interrupt their migrations, the disease has been known to kill large numbers of young salmon.

Acids, Bases, and Water Hardness

Some substances, when added to water, break down in such a way that an acid reaction results. Still other substances have an opposite effect, producing a basic (alkaline) reaction. If the concentrations of acid and base are equal they cancel one another's effects, in which case water or any aqueous solution is said to be neutral. All of this is expressed by a numerical "pH" scale in which neutrality is 7. Any value below 7 indicates an acid reaction (the lower the number the more acid the reaction), whereas basic reactions are expressed by values higher than 7.

Although pH values reported for natural waters have ranged from 2 to 12, the values of most lakes and streams fall between 6.5 and 8.5. Unusually high or low values are often linked with pollution. Some potentially toxic materials are themselves acids or bases, their toxic effects depending largely on the pH of the water. The lethal effects of most acids begin to appear at a pH of about 4.5, while those of most bases show up at around 9.5. For the most part, trout can safely inhabit waters with pH values anywhere between those two extremes.

Water hardness is a result primarily of the presence of calcium (most commonly) and magnesium, and is associated with a high bicarbonate content; the two occur as calcium bicarbonate and magnesium bicarbonate. There is also a relationship between water hardness and pH. Water flowing through forested areas and swampy lowlands tends to be soft and of low pH, largely because of acids produced by decaying vegetation. In regions where limestone is prevalent water is likely to be harder and more alkaline.

Trout production is generally higher in hard waters where the pH is on the high side. In the peat bogs of the upper reaches of Ireland's Liffey River, for instance, the water is soft and has pH values of from 4.6 to 6.8. As it flows along its course the river runs over an area of limestone, where the water becomes harder and the pH rises to from 7.4 to 8.4. In the upstream areas, brown trout normally attain a length of about eight inches at age five; in the harder alkaline waters downstream browns reach that size by age two, and by age five they're about a foot in length. The relationship between trout growth and water conditions apparently isn't direct, but arises instead from the fact that harder waters, being generally richer in nutrients, support larger communities and therefore provide more trout food.

Running Waters

It rains. Or it snows, sleets, or hails. Water thus deposited over the surface of the land may then be taken into the soil to become part of the groundwater, or it may run off the land, swelling rivers and filling lakes. Groundwater also contributes to the flowing and standing waters of the surface, offering stability by dint of its relatively slow but steady seepage into bodies of water. Some water may evaporate back into the atmosphere, and some may be transpired into the air by vegetation whose roots have taken up some of the moisture in the soil. The rest flows into the oceans that cover seven-tenths of the surface of the globe and which, through evaporation, replenish the water content of the atmosphere — making possible more precipitation. The clear water rushing audibly by an angler's waders as he stands in a run is making its way for the nth time through an endless cycle — the so-called hydrologic cycle. And even though the lake water another angler is working is tarrying for a period in one spot, it's only a matter of time before that too will be found elsewhere in the cycle.

Running waters constitute one of the most important of the geologic mechanisms that sculpt the landscape. Powered by gravity, they form their own channels and give rise to valleys. Most of their "energy of fall" is converted into heat energy as water particles rub against one another, against suspended material within the stream and against the stream bed. If, over a particular stretch of water, velocity remains constant, one may conclude that the force of gravity is balanced by frictional resistance.

Turbulence

The flow of water — a force with which organisms living in streams are obliged to spend their lives in continuous battle — may be either laminar or turbulent. In laminar flow, the fluid particles move in parallel layers. But in turbulent flow, which characterizes most naturally flowing waters, the path of a given particle of water is highly irregular and doesn't necessarily conform to the paths of nearby water particles (Figure 5.3). Turbulence is usually greater closer to a stream bed, where velocity, however, is apt to be relatively low — conditions that are reflected in the trout's tendency to hang close to the bottom

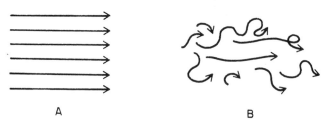

A   B

Figure 5.3. Laminar flow (A) and turbulent flow (B).

when lying in runs. The greatest velocity is found in the upper waters of the deepest portion of a stream (Figure 5.4).

At the same time, there's a thin layer of water immediately in contact with the stream bed in which flow not only is greatly reduced, but also is less turbulent. Moreover, in the interstices between many of the particles making up the bottom, flow is laminar. This condition is important for the survival of numerous bottom-dwelling organisms, which may become trout food.

Obstructions in a current are of more than passing interest to anyone trying to read water for signs of trout. Any object placed in flowing water causes eddies to form on both its upstream and downstream sides (Figure 5.5), and, in these eddies particles swept along on the current may tarry for awhile during their downstream migration, perhaps allowing time for trout to identify them as potential food items. Everything else being equal, larger eddies form around

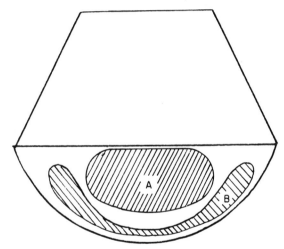

Figure 5.4. Areas of maximum velocity (A) and maximum turbulence (B) in a stream. (Modified from Leighly, 1934.)

Figure 5.5. Eddies formed by an object in flowing water.

larger objects; but around any given object eddies increase in size and in turbulence as water velocity increases. The diffuse nature of eddy turbulence offers respite to trout from the mainstream, so large obstructions almost always provide good trout stations.

In addition to the sundry dissolved substances in water, there's suspended material — fine particulate stuff, usually not more than a fifth of a millimeter in diameter, being swept along by the current. And, there is what goes by the name of bed load, which is made up of all those particles too large to be brought into suspension but small enough to be moved along the stream bed. The downstream movement of the bed load tends to be erratic, with particles rolling, sliding, or perhaps bouncing along and periodically coming to rest.

A stream in flood stage can be an awesome event. Suspended particles act as miniature bullets, chipping away at solid objects. And the shifting of bed materials — sometimes drastic — grinds up large numbers of bottom organisms that might have served as trout fodder. Flooding has traditionally been considered a major enemy by biologists intent on maintaining optimal conditions for trout.

On the other hand, there's evidence that an occasional flood may have some beneficial effects, at least under certain circumstances. Back in June, 1972, for example, James McLaren and his colleagues were in the midst of a study on Pennsylvania's Spruce Creek when tropical storm Agnes hit the area and caused flooding that scoured the creek bed. During May, resident brown trout from 5 to 16 inches long had been captured by electrofishing, and each had been branded with an identification number before being returned to the water. The trout so marked had been placed in three adjacent 700-foot sections, separated from one another by weirs. The flood brought by Agnes removed the weirs. Six weeks following the flood, a survey of the three sections revealed an increase in the total weight of the trout and a slight decrease in their numbers, results that would have been expected under normal conditions as a consequence of growth and average mortality. What is perhaps most surprising is the fact that the recovery of marked trout was even higher in the aftermath of the flood than it had been in two years of average or below average flow for which there were records. It seems that when floods rage, trout either hug the bottom where flow velocities are minimal, or in some way find areas where they are protected from the main thrust of the current.

Under similar conditions eggs deposited in redds don't fare as well, and for this reason a flood of significant proportions may wipe out an entire year class (the individuals hatched in any given year) of trout. The invertebrate organisms of the stream bed, which are eaten by fish, also have their numbers reduced by extremely high water conditions. The browns of Spruce Creek were slimmer following the flood, probably as a result of reduced food supply.

Yet an occasional redistribution of bottom materials probably has a beneficial long term effect on trout populations. Finer sediment, which tends over the years to work into the crevices of gravel, reduces the value of a bottom for spawning because it inhibits the movement of water through the gravel, and so deprives the eggs of oxygen. And, when the interstices between stones are plugged up, the invertebrates normally found there can't thrive. But when a flood hits, it scours the bottom, loosens detrimental sediment and carries it away. When Spruce Creek was surveyed again in 1975, trout production was found to be higher than in any previous year in which surveys had been done.

Not all of the working done to a bottom is beneficial, however. The equipment used in logging operations compacts a bottom, and compaction has the opposite effect of flooding: instead of redistributing the materials, it lodges them even more firmly in place. There's even concern that compaction may be affecting some heavily fished trout streams whose beds are constantly being trampled by the feet of hordes of wading anglers.

Channel Patterns and Falls
Sometimes a stream develops a serpentine or meandering path, especially if it has a bed of loose and relatively fine material — the kind of bed that might be found in a stream in a meadow. Since water naturally crowds to the outside of a bend, it's there that one finds the highest velocity of flow and greatest turbulence (Figure 5.6). The result is maximal erosion at the outside of a meander, and it's there that a high density of trout at feeding stations is likely, because in addition to the invertebrate drift being funneled their way, there's often superior cover close at hand in the form of undercut banks.

Coarser material eroded from the outside of a meander is swept downstream and comes to rest again where the current slows. This means it's usually deposited in the straight stretch preceding the next meander or on the inside of the next meander itself (Figure 5.7). In this way the meandering nature of a stream tends to become more pronounced, and cutoffs may develop which by isolating bends from the mainstream create arclike oxbow lakes (Figure 5.8). Streams that don't really meander may have some of the characteristics of meanders.

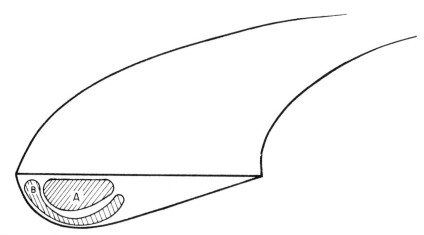

Figure 5.6. A section through a bend in a stream showing displacement to the outside of areas of maximum velocity (A) and maximum turbulence (B). (Modified from Leighly, 1934.)

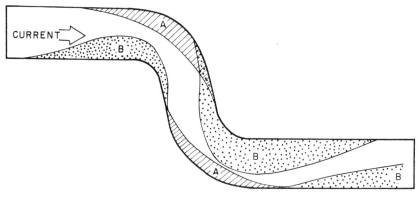

Figure 5.7. Areas of erosion (A) and deposition (B) in bends of a stream. (After Friedkin, 1945.)

Even in a straight river channel, the thalweg (the deepest part of the channel) has a distinct tendency to migrate from one side to another over the length of the watercourse.

Streams with easily eroded banks and major fluctuations in water level may develop a braided pattern. Often such banks are sparsely vegetated and therefore lack the root systems that contribute to soil stability. The pattern begins to develop when midchannel bars (such as sandbars) form under water. The local reductions in water velocity caused by bars lead to the deposition of still more material, the bars enlarge, and ultimately become islands. When high waters recede bars formerly under water are exposed and the braids become more obvious

Figure 5.8. A meandering stretch of Wisconsin's Wolf River. At the top of the photo an ox-bow cutoff can be seen. (Courtesy of Nils Meland, University of Wisconsin, Oshkosh.)

Figure 5.9. A braided stream, the Swanson River of British Columbia. The high country in the background is the Juneau Ice Field through which runs the Alaska-B.C. boundary. (Courtesy of Thomas Laudon, Geology Department, University of Wisconsin, Oshkosh.)

(Figure 5.9). Where currents passing on either side of a bar come together downstream, the effect is like the confluence of two streams, and the combined currents carry drifting food into a long and fairly narrow strip that provides plenty of feeding stations for trout.

The sudden vertical drop at a waterfall allows water to develop substantial velocity, and this causes a plunge pool to form at the base of the falls. Turbulence in a plunge pool undercuts this base, and the undercutting increases the likelihood of caving beneath the falls (Figure 5.10). By this process falls tend, over a long period, to erode their way upstream. Plunge pools are typically deep, offering excellent feeding stations in quiet waters next to turbulent areas, and undercut areas often provide some of the most well-protected stations within a stream.

Lakes

Lakes are essentially depressions in the earth's crust in which water is temporarily delayed in its progress toward the sea. They are complex systems with various zones, currents, and other features that trout respond to. Whereas stream water contains a relative abundance of suspended matter, lake water, because of comparative lack of motion, allows sediments to settle. Lakes therefore act as settling basins and are constantly in the process of filling in.

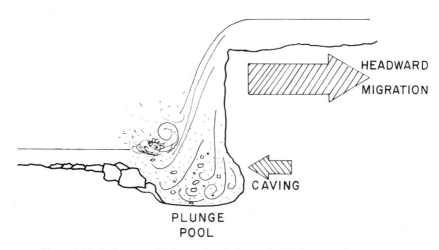

Figure 5.10. A plunge pool is formed at the base of a falls by water hitting at high velocity. Particulate matter, moved at high speeds in the turbulent water, helps in digging out the pool and in caving. Over time, the falls migrates in a headward direction.

Zonation

Lakes possess definable zones, in any of which trout may be found. Closest to shore is a littoral zone into which enough light penetrates to permit the presence of rooted vegetation (Figure 5.11). A littoral area can vary considerably in width, and a shallow pond may be entirely littoral in character. Where shores are well protected from wind and wave action the littoral zone might be subdivided: an area of emergent vegetation would be closest to the shoreline; beyond that there might be plants with floating leaves; and farther out there would be a region of submerged vegetation extending as far as the compensation depth — that depth at which the amount of light is just sufficient to allow plants to maintain themselves. The littoral zone generally produces a greater amount of living tissue per unit of volume than any other zone in a lake. Its large plants provide habitats for animals and sometimes the only real trout cover in a lake; as a rule, there are more resident animal species in the littoral zone than elsewhere.

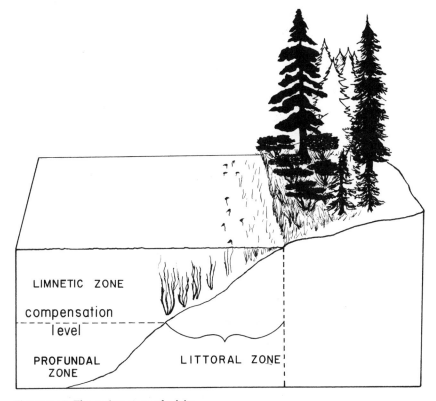

Figure 5.11. The major zones of a lake.

The limnetic zone is the area of open water beyond the littoral zone that extends from the surface downward to the compensation depth. Since light can penetrate this zone, it's characterized by an abundance of planktonic organisms (small organisms that depend upon currents for their distribution). Extending from the lower boundary of the limnetic zone all the way to the lake bottom is the profundal zone — the deepest part of the lake, as the name suggests. Because of the insufficient light here plant production doesn't take place, but many of the organic materials produced in the limnetic zone drift downward, so the profundal zone really isn't a desert. Bottom sediments are inhabited by decomposer organisms that break down plant and animal tissues.

Stratification

In winter, when ice covers are found on northern lakes, the water immediately beneath the ice is close to the freezing point of 0 °C. From that point downward the water becomes a bit warmer until, in the vicinity of the bottom, it's generally at or near 4 °C, the temperature at which water is heaviest (Figure 5.12).

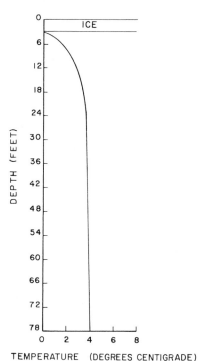

Figure 5.12. Typical water temperatures for a temperate lake in winter.

With the onset of warm weather the ice melts, and spring winds stir circulation within the entire body of water, distributing nutrients in the process. The toxic gases of decomposition, which become concentrated close to the bottom during the winter, are brought into surface waters, where they diffuse out into the atmosphere. At the same time, atmospheric oxygen is taken into the lake water, which may have been depleted of some oxygen during the winter. The whole process, known as the spring overturn, has been compared to taking a deep breath, and the analogy is a good one. The overturn provides respite for trout and other creatures that may have been existing under the ice sheet in stress-producing or even near-lethal conditions of oxygen deprivation.

As hotter weather approaches the surface water heats up, making it lighter than the colder layers beneath. This difference in density impedes the mixing of the layers, and the process, once begun, continues until the surface waters are warm enough and sufficiently lighter than the lower strata to prevent the mixing of the entire lake under normal wind conditions. Circulation then becomes confined to the surface waters. And as the heat of summer increases surface temperatures still further, the density differences between the waters of the upper and lower portions of the lake become even more pronounced. This layering constitutes the phenomenon known as thermal stratification; the upper portion is called the epilimnion, the lower portion the hypolimnion, and the transition layer between the two the thermocline. The latter is characterized by a profound drop in temperature between its upper and lower edges (Figure 5.13). Frequently, the thermocline is so sharply defined that an underwater swimmer in the epilimnion can detect the changes if he plunges an arm through the thermocline into the hypolimnion below.

Wind conditions play a dominant role in thermal stratification. Stratification may be disrupted by the agitation caused by high winds, and in any given year prolonged or recurring strong winds may prevent stratification from taking place at all. Once stratification has begun, however, resistance to mixing increases as the densities of the epilimnion and hypolimnion waters become more widely divergent.

Throughout the summer significant circulation in a stratified lake is normally confined to the epilimnion. There also, water temperatures may fluctuate according to the dictates of the weather. However, the hypolimnion, isolated beneath the thermocline, remains essentially at a constant temperature. Cut off from the agitating influence of wind, movement within its water mass is slight. Its isolation also prevents it

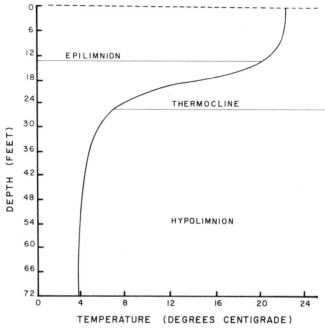

Figure 5.13. Typical temperature distributions in a thermally stratified lake.

from receiving oxygen from the atmosphere, so as organic decomposition continues the oxygen level of hypolimnion water decreases and the waste products of decomposition build up. A thermally stratified lake is therefore said to be undergoing a summer stagnation.

In relatively shallow ponds with their hypolimnions of smaller volume, oxygen sometimes becomes so scarce that the creatures living in the hypolimnion asphyxiate. "Summerkill" is the term used when large numbers of them die in this way. In lakes of great depth, hypolimnions are usually voluminous enough to offset the dangers posed by changes in dissolved oxygen and the accumulated products of decomposition. Such lakes are more favorable for salmonids.

If oxygen in the hypolimnion decreases to a level unfavorable to salmonids, these fish may be found moving into epilimnion waters for short periods, even though temperatures there may be uncomfortably high for them. For limited periods salmonids can tolerate high temperatures that would kill them over a long span of time. They may also remain in shallow water if there's an influx of colder water from a spring or some similar source.

Decreases in air temperature that come in the autumn cool the waters of the epilimnion. And as surface strata are cooled, their water becomes heavier and sinks so that warmer, lighter water is brought to the surface where it, in turn, is cooled. This exchange constitutes mixing by convection, and the currents thus produced are called convection currents. The process continues until the thermocline has been eroded away, and wind action can then effect the complete circulation of lake water characteristic of the fall overturn. Aeration of the water and nutrient distribution result, as in the spring overturn. Eventually, the entire lake cools to a uniform 4 °C — or approximately so — from top to bottom. Surface water cooled further by colder air then remains on top, since it's lighter.

When an ice sheet forms the underlying water is naturally shielded, so conditions under the ice come to resemble those of the hypolimnion in summer. Organic decomposition makes inroads on the available supply of oxygen and causes decomposition products to collect. The lake then experiences winter stagnation. Since light penetrates the ice, except under conditions of substantial snow cover, photosynthesis generally proceeds all winter. But as decomposition from the bottom continues, the region of poorly oxygenated water enlarges and encroaches upon the upper photosynthetic zone; as a result, trout may be forced up closer to the ice sheet as winter progresses. Sometimes the oxygen level falls too low, causing the high mortalities known as winterkill.

Currents and Seiches

There are currents in lakes: horizontal currents caused by play of winds across water surfaces and the comings and goings of water at inlets and outlets; and vertical currents caused by upwellings from such deep sources as springs or by deflections of horizontal currents by bottom formations. The convection currents characteristic of seasonal overturns are essentially vertical in nature.

Sometimes winds pile surface water onto a lee shore, raising the water level there and creating a return current that flows away from the shore and below the surface current. The layer between the two currents, the shearing plane, is stationary. If stratification hasn't occurred the returning current will probably flow close to the bottom, but if stratification has taken place it will flow along the upper portion of the thermocline. When it does this, friction from the returning current may cause enough motion within the thermocline itself to transmit some motion to the hypolimnion, creating slight currents there (Figure 5.14).

Seiches are periodic variations in water level analogous to the to-

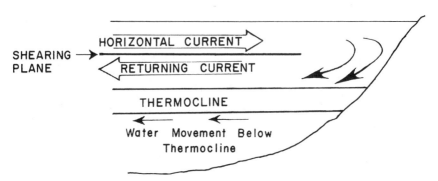

Figure 5.14. A wind-caused horizontal current with a returning current below it.

and-fro oscillations of water set in motion by a body in a tub. In lakes the force that most commonly gives rise to seiches is a strong wind of short duration, although local variations in atmospheric pressure or rainfall may also bring them on. Water suddenly piled up on one shore naturally causes a rise in the water level there, and when the force that caused the change in the water level is released, the lake water begins to swing back and forth. The time required for an oscillation depends on the size and contour of the lake basin, while the variation in water level depends upon the magnitude of the initial force as well as on the size of the lake. In large lakes water levels during a seiche may vary by as much as several feet (in rare cases), but in lakes of moderate size the variations are usually too small to be noticed unless they are looked for.

When a thermocline is present, a subsurface seiche may occur when seiche-producing forces cause water to pile up on one side of the

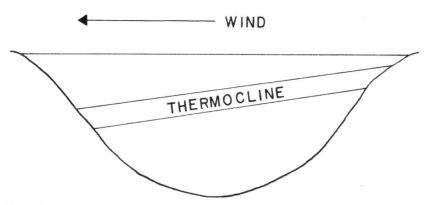

Figure 5.15. A subsurface seiche.

lake, exerting force on the thermocline and forcing it downward; simultaneously, the thermocline rises on the opposite side of the lake (Figure 5.15). When the original force is removed, the thermocline swings back and forth in gradually decreasing oscillations until equilibrium is again established.

Fishing in unfamiliar lakes can be discouraging, one reason being that lake currents aren't read with the same ease as currents in streams. But currents in lakes may have a strong bearing on local temperatures and on the distribution of dissolved substances and therefore on the distribution of salmonids and other aquatic organisms. Seiches, because they lead to variations in the depth of the thermocline, can also alter fish distribution. Experienced anglers find it useful to lower a thermometer into the water to learn where a radical temperature change may be before going about the business of fishing.

Lake Productivity

The basis for the most universally accepted classification of lakes involves biological productivity. Lakes categorized as oligotrophic (literally, "scant nutrition") are low in the concentrations of nutrients needed for plant growth, like nitrates and phosphates. Such lakes possess minimal amounts of decomposing organic debris, and they're typically deep, have steep bottoms, and are cold and well oxygenated in all zones (Figure 5.16). Since oligotrophic lakes best fulfill the physical needs of salmonids, the classic trout lakes fall within this category.

Eutrophic lakes (i.e., "good nutrition"), by contrast, are rich in dissolved nutrients and have significant bottom deposits of organic matter. They're shallower and warmer than oligotrophic lakes, and have a greater abundance of rooted vegetation in their marginal areas (Figure 5.17). Dissolved oxygen is plentiful in these vegetated areas, but in other areas it is a lot lower than in oligotrophic lakes.

As the names imply, eutrophic lakes are the more productive of the two. Because they possess such an abundance of nutrients, plant life thrives, and the production of animal tissue follows suit. Though some oligotrophic lakes may yield trophy-sized trout, they are physically incapable of producing the sheer mass of tissue per acre for a given time period that can be produced by a eutrophic lake.

A lake typically begins its existence in an oligotrophic condition, and as time passes and sediments accumulate it becomes more eutrophic. Although there are some exceptions, eutrophication is in progress in nearly all lakes. The rate of the process varies from one body of water to another, and the activities of man have tended to ac-

Figure 5.16. The shoreline of a large northern oligotrophic lake — deep, clear, with a rocky shoreline, and relatively low in the production of organic material for a given area. (Courtesy of William Sloey, University of Wisconsin, Oshkosh.)

Figure 5.17. This small Wisconsin pond is typical of a eutrophic body of water. It is shallow and heavily vegetated. For a given area, such a body of water is biologically more productive than an oligotrophic lake or pond. (Courtesy of William Sloey, University of Wisconsin, Oshkosh.)

celerate it considerably. As the transition is made from oligotrophic to eutrophic conditions, there's a shift in species composition from salmonids and other cold-water creatures to warm-water species that are better able to cope with higher temperatures and lower levels of dissolved oxygen. And rather than being an end in itself, a eutrophic lake, like an oligotrophic lake, is destined to pass from the scene: the process of filling with sediment continues until the lake becomes extinct — and terrestrial habitats are established. As all of this transpires, though, movement in the earth's crust and the various actions of glaciers and rivers are creating basins for future lakes. Even as some lakes are in the process of dying, others are being born.

The aquatic medium is part of the trout's environment and it supports the plants and animals that make up the community in which the trout lives. The behavior of trout and how they interact with the community is the subject of the next two chapters.

6.
Nonreproductive Behavior

Behavior aids survival; conversely, survival considerations shape behavior.
—GLENN E. WEISFELD, 1977

Information about trout behavior is scattered here and there throughout biological literature, much of it hidden within writings dealing with other aspects of these fish. Some of it is conflicting; a number of studies have involved only immature fish; and for the many observations made under laboratory conditions, it's difficult to say to what extent inferences can be made for wild populations. Nevertheless, behavior patterns appear to be similar for the various salmonid species, and when putting together the results of many observations, from the field and from the lab, a fairly coherent picture emerges.

Territoriality

Among stream-dwelling salmonids there exists social order. Individual fish are territorial in that they occupy specific areas which they defend against intruders; this defense involves a spectrum of aggressive behavior patterns. The territory is essentially a feeding area, and within it there is, according to most accounts, a single spot, the "station," from which the territory is defended and feeding excursions are made (Figure 6.1). There are some reports of multiple stations maintained by a single individual within well-defined territories.

The size of a given territory is usually difficult to pinpoint exactly, but estimates have been made by recording the points at which occupants become aggressive toward intruders. In general, territory size is directly correlated with the size of the fish. Atlantic salmon fry of perhaps a few inches in length hold territories of 30-50 square inches, while one nine-inch brown trout is known to have had a territory estimated at something like four square yards.

Territory size can also depend upon the degree of visual isolation among individuals; bottom contours, vegetation, logs, increased tur-

128

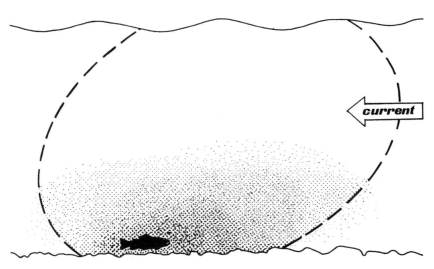

Figure 6.1. A side view of a territory of a young Atlantic salmon or brown trout. The broken line shows the feeding range, while the shading indicates centrifugally decreasing aggressiveness. (Redrawn from Harry Kalleberg, *Observations in a Stream Tank of Territoriality and Competition in Juvenile Salmon and Trout [Salmo solar L. and S. trutta L.]* Institute of Freshwater Research, Report no. 39, Drottningholm, 1958, pp. 55-99.)

bidity, and other factors that obscure adjacent individuals from one another may allow a greater density of fish in an area and, consequently, smaller territories (Figure 6.2). A territory is usually defended with increasing vigor as the distance from the station decreases, and between two neighboring territories there may be a transition zone which is of interest to the occupants of each territory.

Territorial boundaries tend to be more distinct where there is a pronounced bottom contour. Obvious topographic features such as rocks are used as visual references, and while an intruder is usually safe from aggression while on the far side of such an object, it will normally provoke an attack or a threat display if it crosses the reference point.

Salmonids feed predominantly upon organic drift, almost exclusively in the form of prey animals. At their stations, salmonids face directly into the current, and the stations, ideally, are situated to allow a good view of material being swept downstream while simultaneously affording cover and protection from the buffeting effects of the current. The ideal station permits a maximal food intake while requiring a minimal expenditure of energy to maintain the position. Within the territory, stations are usually located in a pocket, over a rise in the bottom, in the water cushion in front of rocks, or just downstream from rocks or

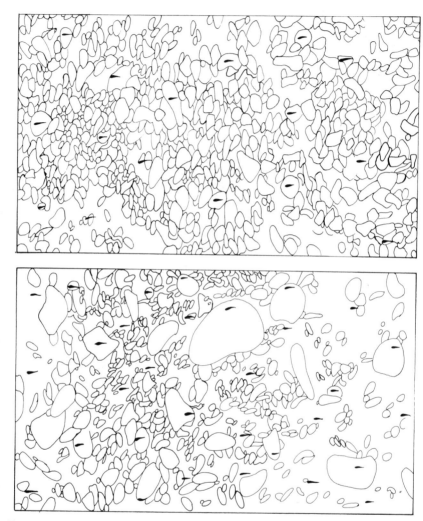

Figure 6.2. These figures demonstrate the effect of bottom topography on the size of territories of Atlantic salmon fry. The more irregular topography (bottom), in allowing visual isolation between individuals, permits smaller territories and, therefore, a greater density of fish. Kalleberg determined the average territory size in the upper mosaic to be 9.2 square decimeters, and that in the lower mosaic to be 4.5 square decimeters. (Redrawn from Kalleberg, 1958.)

other objects — places in which the fish are able to escape the main thrust of the current. The strength of a position is also affected by water depth, darkness, and shade.

A station is apparently chosen with some stable object or surface as a reference point, because its location is reported to be constant to within a fraction of an inch. When a trout departs from its station to make a feeding excursion, it returns to *precisely* the same spot. Where currents are strong enough to buffet a fish about the axes of the eyes maintain a constant direction, so that the nose remains relatively stationary while the rest of the body oscillates. It has been said that this behavior produces the impression of the fish being suspended in the current, the eyeballs acting as universal joints.

Within a territory there may also be refuge positions where trout go when frightened or when chased by larger members of their own kind. Occasionally — especially during the middle of the day — trout retire to a refuge to go through an inactive period of variable duration. Refuge positions are located in such secluded places as the hollows beneath rocks or undercut banks and appear to be chosen for the maximum protection they afford.

Areas of streams inhabited by very young salmonids can be viewed as a series of adjacent territories, each occupied by a single individual. The pattern thus produced is a territorial mosaic. Figure 6.3 shows the relative sizes of the territories in a mosaic of young Atlantic salmon; the boundaries, not perfectly symmetrical, were determined by recording the aggressive contacts between occupants.

There is evidence that in order for classic mosaic patterns to form, a certain uniformity in the size of the individual fish is necessary, as well as some uniformity in the character of the stream bottom; the fish must also remain in their territories rather than change locations often. These conditions are found among very young fish and in the

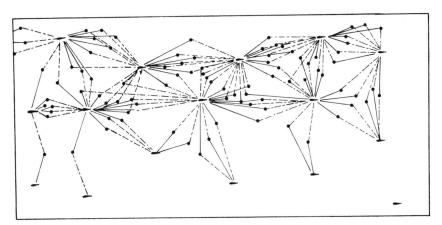

Figure 6.3. The black spots show the locations of observed "aggressive contacts" between Atlantic salmon fry in a territorial mosaic. Unbroken lines show movement toward intruders (i.e., by defenders), while broken lines indicate movement toward defenders. (After Kalleberg, 1958.)

nursery areas they inhabit and, perhaps (but rarely) in areas where the population is very sparse. Normally, when fish begin to grow larger, definite social groupings develop, as will be discussed later.

Even within mosaics, territorial changes do take place from time to time, because as a fish grows so does its need for more space. Neighboring fish too are growing and increasing their territorial needs, so pressure from local competition acts as an impetus for movement to a less competitive location. And the competition is stiff from the very beginning. Individuals that have been able to establish and defend the best territories (feeding areas) grow more rapidly, while those forced into poorer locations, where cover and food supply are perhaps suboptimal, are less fit and therefore more susceptible to predation and disease.

As trout get older they begin to move away from the nursery areas where they spent their early lives. There is a broad spectrum of habitats in a typical trout stream, and naturally fish move into the areas that especially meet their requirements. There is no evidence that any intrinsic social nature acts to bring trout together; rather, it is the physically desirable aspects of some areas that draw them. And as small fish grow and move into these areas, their old territorial mosaics break down.

Within the desirable areas the type of social structure that develops is hierarchical; some authors call it a "nipping-order." From all appearances, rank within the order depends almost exclusively on size. Hierarchies are also characterized by partial territoriality — within the areas they inhabit, stations are held by different trout at different times.

In streams in which flood conditions and the resulting redistribution of bottom materials are common occurrences, many old territories become unrecognizable. In recently flooded streams, therefore, a lot of fish have to establish new territories.

But the strong territoriality so characteristic of salmonids in running water virtually disappears where there's no current. As water velocity decreases and finally approaches zero, mature fish begin to move about in a random way and on an individual basis. Young fish, on the other hand, replace their territorial behavior with a tendency to school.

Agonistic Behavior

Agonistic behavior is the term applied to the collection of reactions involving threat, attack, and flight from attack. Agonistic behavior patterns are pretty much the same for all salmonids. Although one species might show a greater degree of aggressiveness than another, or might exhibit some slight variation in motion when carrying out an act, the fundamental character of each action is surprisingly similar from one species to another.

Agonistic behavior elicits color changes in some species of salmonids. Young Atlantic salmon, for instance, become lighter when in a dominant role, but darken when in a subordinate role. Brook trout reportedly brighten during a threat display, but rainbows don't exhibit the same effect. On the other hand, both brookies and rainbows darken when being chased.

There isn't much agreement among observers as to when agonistic behavior is most common during the day. Some observers report a decrease during periods of active feeding, but others report that trout become more aggressive toward evening, just as the feeding rate is also on the rise. In any event, an act of aggression is likely to precipitate a period of instability within the social order, so that other aggressive acts may follow. Then there's a period of relative calm.

Frontal Threat Display

The frontal threat display (Figure 6.4) is made by aggressive fish while swimming forward. As the fish approaches an opponent, it fixes the opponent with its eyes and arches its back; all fins are fully extended, except the dorsal, and the gill covers are flared out. The mouth is open, and the floor of the mouth is forced downward to give the mouth a pouchlike shape. In a head-on view the fish appears to increase in size in much the same way as an angry dog with its hair standing up. A frontal threat display generally lasts only a few seconds, and commonly ends with an attack.

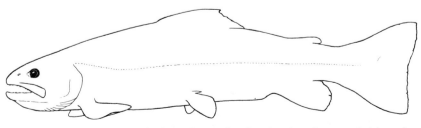

Figure 6.4. Frontal threat display. (Composite drawing based on a sketch and a photograph by Kalleberg, 1958.)

Many animal behaviorists think that threat displays in general result from a conflict between drives to attack and to flee. The extended fins in the frontal threat display have been associated by some with braking motions and thus with the drive to escape, but everyone agrees that it's basically aggressive in nature.

Lateral Threat Display

The lateral threat display (Figure 6.5) is so named because a displaying fish turns its flanks toward its opponent. The body is stretched out, with the line of the back fairly straight and the lateral line upwardly concave. This display has been described as resembling a spasm, since fish in the lateral display posture appear to be rigid and may even vibrate. All fins are fully extended, and there is some dilation of the mouth and gill region. Sometimes there's an oscillation of the body about the vertical axis, which some authors call a "wig-wag display." Wig-wag displays may be performed with the head tilted down, but rarely with the head up.

If a territory holder reacts to an intrusion by giving a lateral display, and if this fails to frighten the intruder away, the intensity of the display may be increased so that a similar display from the intruder is provoked. In mutual lateral threat displays the two fish, positioned parallel to one another and facing upstream, may vibrate with such intensity that they actually move upstream. There has been at least one observation of fish that were so thoroughly occupied with their display that they entered the territory of a third fish, which joined in the display. If the vibration is less intense the fish may remain stationary or even move downstream. Lateral displays apparently don't carry as much aggressive intent as frontal displays, and may even indicate a measure of submission. Although they might result in an attack by one fish or the other, they often simply come to an uneventful end.

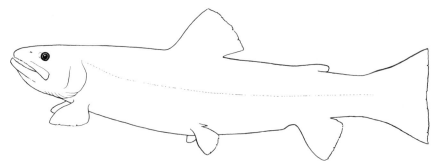

Figure 6.5. Lateral threat display. (Modified from Kalleberg, 1958.)

Direct Attack (Charge)
The charge is the most direct form of aggression. A charging fish fixes its adversary optically, raises the dorsal fin slightly, and swims with rapid strokes of the tail toward its target victim. The paired fins are held close to the body. A charge usually ends with the attacker nipping the other fish.

Biting
A bite is the normal end product of a charge or of an attack following a frontal threat display. Most bites are directed toward the tail region — either the caudal fin or the caudal peduncle — but this might simply be a result of the fact that the most available portion of a fleeing fish is its posterior. Other fins may be bitten too, and if an attacker gets a solid grip it may hold on and shake. Less often the snout and back are bitten, and when an attacked fish counterattacks rather than yields, the sides are favored targets. But unless prolonged combat develops, serious damage usually isn't sustained.

Flight and Appeasement
Although flight may be preceded by a lateral threat display, a trout normally flees once attacked. A trout in flight swims rapidly with its fins tucked in close to its body, it's apparent intent simply to vacate the vicinity. Such flight might cause an aggressor to change a slow approach to a charge, or it might terminate the encounter altogether.

Appeasement refers to the tendency of a trout to drop motionless to the bottom when approached by a larger individual. Smaller fish feeding on the downstream side of a large fish sometimes maintain their positions by dropping in this manner when threatened. The larger trout might stand by for several seconds with its nose practically touching a smaller trout, but the latter can usually resume its feeding once the former has turned away.

The Tail-first Approach
When a fish floats passively downstream toward the position held by another individual it is said to be using the tail-first approach. The fish thus approached also backs downstream, the end result being that it gets displaced. There's no apparent indication either of aggressive intent or of submission during the encounter.

Combat
Salmonids of all ages engage in genuine combat. When neither fish gives way during an encounter, long bouts of pushing, ramming and rapid biting may result. Some combatants circle one another, biting and

shaking furiously for several seconds if a sufficient hold can be maintained on an extremity. If the fighting is violent surface wounds may be inflicted, fins may be damaged, and scales lost. Occasionally, fighting brook trout have been reported to strike one another with their flanks while circling one another.

It's possible that real combat is more frequent at certain ages than at others. Atlantic salmon fry, for example, fight frequently, but in older parr agonistic behavior usually takes the form of display activity. And adult salmon, unless they're spawning, also tend toward display rather than combat.

Hierarchies

When trout grow and leave nursery areas, they gather in specific locales and form natural groupings that are dominance hierarchies — relatively stable social orders in which nip rights prevail. That certain parts of a stream attract such groupings is associated with the drift patterns in the stream (Figure 6.6). The stations defended are usually beneath the principal currents (which concentrate drifting food) but only if they provide some protection from the current's force. Desirable positions are close to cover, and it appears that soon after occupying a territory a trout develops a strategy for making a rapid escape. Regardless of the nature of the cover — a rock, an undercut bank — a fish heads for it quickly when danger threatens.

The dominant individual in a hierarchy has its choice of stations and certainly takes the best one available. Subordinate fish take positions of lesser advantage. But within hierarchies the best positions aren't always held by the same trout; rather, there's a kind of rotation in "ownership." Although a large trout will normally defend its territory of the moment successfully against a smaller intruder, a larger intruder may force it to yield. If a choice territory is vacated temporarily, a smaller trout, which has been in a lesser territory will soon take the better spot; the territory left open by the smaller trout will in turn be occupied by a still smaller trout — and so it can go, like a small chain reaction. Such position changes aren't necessarily taking place all the time, and some trout can be seen at the same station all day while others may change stations a number of times.

One of the best studies of trout behavior to have been done was made by Thomas Jenkins, a doctoral student at the University of California. By watching browns and rainbows from elevated viewing

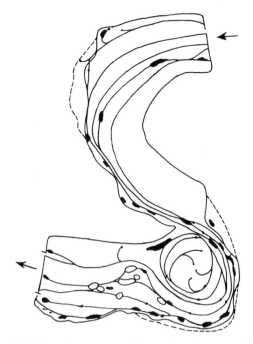

Figure 6.6. The principle surface currents in a section of stream. Feeding positions are shown as solid black. (Redrawn from Jenkins, 1969.)

posts, he found that stations used by the trout could be divided into two categories: "*a* positions" were frequented by dominant fish and by subordinates if dominants left them vacant; "*b* positions" were used by subordinates but never by dominants. By discovering and recording the movement patterns of trout between feeding stations, Jenkins was able to define broad stream areas which might encompass many stations (Figure 6.7). "*A* areas" contained *a* positions, while "*B* areas" contained *b* positions. *A* areas were centers of activity because dominant trout located there. Subordinates might take up positions in an *A* area when the dominant fish was in an upstream position within the area, or perhaps elsewhere in hiding, but they would eventually be driven off with the return of the dominant fish.

In general, aggressiveness and dominance are based on size, with larger trout being more aggressive and hence more dominant, as you'd expect. If age and sex have any effects, they are masked by sheer size. But ranking within hierarchies does have its imperfections, because a subordinate sometimes attacks a more dominant fish with success. As a matter of fact, the social units of trout have been described as hierarchies "with infrequent subordinate revolt." Dominance relations be-

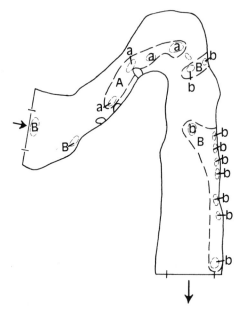

Figure 6.7. The relationships between feeding areas and positions in a section of stream. (Redrawn from Jenkins, 1969.)

tween trout of about equal size don't appear to be secure, so a lot of the conflict that takes place in an area may be between such near-equal individuals.

Prior residence in a territory enhances a trout's aggressiveness, and fish that are aggressive while defending their own territories will flee if attacked in the territory of another. In experiments in which new trout have been introduced into established hierarchies, aggressive actions were invariably initiated by resident fish, even though they might be smaller than the new fish. Since a stream area is defended by all members of a hierarchy, it's possible that a kind of collective advantage exists in favor of the resident trout.

All trout streams have some transient fish that don't belong to a recognizable hierarchy and that don't hold stable positions from one hour to the next. Sometimes transient fish form aggregations at the entrances to pools; such aggregations are characterized by frequent threat displays and a general absence of settled relationships. Transient fish are at an aggressive disadvantage when in areas held by hierarchies, but on rare occasions a persistent transient may gain entry into a hierarchy.

It's possible that among fish of very large size territoriality may decrease because big fish sometimes move constantly rather than settle into a position in the current. Such fish seem to prefer scavenging and feeding on fish rather than on organic drift. And even though they might be found in the vicinity of collections of transients, they rarely display signs of agonistic behavior.

Not surprisingly, social rank and agonistic behavior are modified by disease or injury. If subjected to electrofishing, trout show practically no signs of normal aggression for several days and their rank within a hierarchy decreases. In some cases they neither flee nor display, even when bitten by an attacker; but such effects are temporary. When fish become infected with fungus, their social rank decreases as their disease progresses.

Movement

Occasionally trout depart from their stations in the middle of the day to wander about in a seemingly aimless manner. And in pools where there are fish belonging to no recognizable hierarchy, a trout might periodically make a short patrol around the pool perimeter. But in both wandering and patrolling, movement is strictly local rather than long-range.

Most studies of salmonids in stream habitats support the view that these fish refrain from making long-range movements. Although they might travel many hundreds of yards to spawn, there's evidence that they return to their old haunts after spawning is completed. Trout probably spend their lives within a stretch of just a few hundred feet.

Some studies indicate that nonreproductive migration takes place among some salmonid populations. In a notable experiment, tagged brook and brown trout were released in Michigan's famed Au Sable River system. Between 10 and 20 percent of the recaptured trout had migrated up to 10 miles from their point of release. But it's worthy of note that the fish had been collected by shocking them, and that they were anesthetized for tagging. Such treatment can modify behavior in trout, and in this case it might have induced some of them to migrate. The consensus among biologists appears to be that trout normally stay at home and don't move around looking for better accommodations.

Relationships between Species

The different species of trout, salmon, and char have agonistic behavior patterns that are virtually identical, so it isn't surprising that they understand one another's threat displays. Members of several species often make up a single hierarchy, and they can threaten one another, develop dominance-subordination relationships, and defend territories without apparent regard for species differences. Nip rights are based primarily on size: a large rainbow may dominate a small brookie, and a large brookie a small rainbow. In terms of nonreproductive behavior, these fish may act as a single species.

Many non-salmonid fish confine their agonistic behavior to members of their own species, but some salmonids have been seen to defend their territories against virtually all fish not appreciably larger than themselves. Non-salmonids react to attack from salmonids and to frontal threat display (both of which are pretty direct), but don't appear to understand what a lateral threat display is all about.

Although salmonids have similar agonistic behavior patterns, some species are more aggressive than others. When two species cohabit, the one behaving less aggressively (assuming that sizes are about the same) tends to have the less desirable territories. Brook trout, for instance, are known to be especially aggressive, and in lab experiments involving young brookies and Atlantic salmon the brook trout so dominated the salmon that the latter actually avoided desirable shaded areas held by the trout. Brown trout parr display with greater intensity than do Atlantic salmon parr, with the apparent result that their displays carry a greater threat value. So the dominance of salmon by browns is favored.

Domestication and Behavior

Domestication — long-term selective breeding — can yield strains of trout that behave differently than wild strains do. This really isn't surprising, because breeding stock for domestic strains would certainly be chosen on the basis of identifiable physical traits rather than behavioral characteristics.

In one study which compared wild brook trout with a strain of brookies that had undergone domestication for about 90 years, study fish were reared in adjacent troughs and under identical conditions to preclude the effects of environmental influences. Throughout the study, domestic fish were less wary than wild fish, tended to conceal themselves less, and to move toward the surface more frequently. And when the trout were moved from the troughs into pond or stream conditions, domestic fish had a lower survival rate. Even after four months living in natural conditions the domestic trout had acquired little in the way of wariness. Quite aside from these behavioral differences, the wild fish could withstand greater concentrations of accumulated metabolites, as well as higher temperatures. In tests designed to keep fish swimming until signs of exhaustion were visible, domestic fish were shown to have less stamina.

Other comparison experiments have yielded similar results, but this is not to say that all domestic strains of trout are going to behave absolutely identically. It simply points out that there may be some differences between wild and domestic fish. And it's fair to assume the differences usually won't favor the survival of domestic fish as much as they do wild fish.

Feeding Behavior

Salmonids in streams spend most of their time at their stations scanning the current for the drifting prey animals that make up the bulk of their diet. From time to time a fish will dart quickly upstream or to one side, grab a prey item with a sudden turn, and return promptly to its station, where it may or may not mouth the food before swallowing it. Or a fish may rise to the surface to suck in a floater. Sometimes a fish takes prey from the bottom, though less often as a rule. Most of these forays from the station include distances from just a few inches to a foot or so, but there can be departures of a yard or more, in which case a trout might interact with another fish, or even make a change in station.

Salmonids learn to distinguish among the various items that come tumbling along in the current. Fry recently emerged from the gravel at first take in all kinds of sundry debris, even air bubbles. But after a few weeks the ability to distinguish between edibles and nonedibles improves.

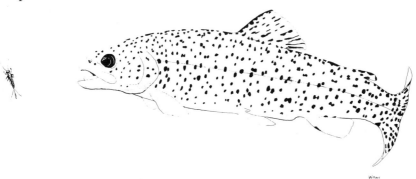

Figure 6.8. Trout and prey.

The initial perception of prey, as well as prey capture, is apparently done chiefly on a visual basis, and it's widely held that visual stimuli are of prime importance in eliciting feeding activity. But it's probable that many last minute rejections of potential foods are made on the basis of odor. Sometimes food is spit out one or more times and then taken in again, or finally rejected. In addition to possessing excellent powers of olfaction, salmonids apparently have an acute gustatory sense, so some rejections may be made on the basis of taste.

Trout sometimes resort to literally chewing up some bigger animals such as crayfish. And they may also shake their prey with a violent jerking of the head from side to side. The shaking routine is most common when prey is too large to be swallowed easily, but it isn't confined to large prey alone, since trout occasionally go through vigorous prey-shaking motions after ingesting some minute morsel. Prey-shaking may even take place after a fish has missed its prey altogether.

In the evening, if surface-feeding activity is intense, trout may not return to their stations near the bottom between forays to the surface, but may move out into open water. They may then temporarily leave their territories altogether in what amounts to a short feeding migration, perhaps to some nearby pool. Usually they are less wary during such periods. Surface-feeding fish can sometimes capture slow-flying insects on the wing at distances beyond a foot above the surface. This activity indicates fine accuracy and coordination, but more than that, it reveals an ability to correct for the bending of light rays at the air-water interface.

The diurnal rhythms in salmonids are well known. Usually, the greatest feeding activity is observed during mornings and evenings, with less activity seen during the middle of the day. As darkness approaches feeding picks up, peaking perhaps around sunset, and then tapering off until it terminates with darkness.

Inactivity at night has been reported for many, perhaps most, salmonid species, including brown trout. But many anglers would disagree with the inclusion of browns, because night fishing for browns constitutes some of the best angling offered in many areas. The truth of the matter is that reports of night-feeding browns are conflicting. One study concluded not only that they're more active at night, but also that they're more active in continuous darkness than in continuous daylight — that light depresses their activity. But another study, in which five brown trout were constantly monitored for activity, demonstrated that four of the fish were active during the day, while during the summer one offbeat individual was more active at night. Just one of the five. Drawing attention to this study — and to this fish — is worthwhile, because it illustrates the kind of variation that can sometimes exist between individuals of the same species. It's interesting to speculate about the degree to which the genetic strain may determine behavior such as night activity.

The amount of food in the stomach at any given time helps determine how hungry a fish may be, so the quantity of food that a trout consumes over a given period hinges upon the speed with which the stomach is evacuated. Salmonids are cold-blooded, so their rate of metabolism (digestion included) depends upon the water temperature. In very cold water, the digestive process slows and the stomach empties more slowly, which would seem to indicate that in warmer water digestion would be faster and the fish would eat more. But salmonids, being cold-water fish, tend not to feed as well when the water gets too warm. The appetites of young sockeye salmon, for example, are at a maximum at water temperatures of about 15-16 °C. At that temperature digestion proceeds at about 75 percent of its maximum rate; at 5 °C the process is so slow that the fish probably wouldn't have to eat much more often than once a week.

Characteristics of the food itself may also affect the evacuation rate of the stomach. Foods with a high fat content tend to slow the process, and so do big prey animals with heavy exoskeletons, such as crayfish. Larger pieces of exoskeleton have to remain in the stomach to soften before they can pass into the intestine. On the other hand, the sheer size of a meal doesn't appear to affect the emptying rate of the stomach very much.

It's known that food specialization may occur in trout — that certain individuals within a population may prefer certain types of prey. But specializations aren't permanent — they change periodically. According to reports, specialized food preferences are more pronounced over short periods of time, although they may last as long as six months. There seem to be no strong correlations between the degree of specialization and the size, growth rate, or earlier preferences of the individual fish. (See the sections ''Food Pyramids'' and ''Foods consumed by Trout'' in Chapter 8).

Familiarity with a food can stimulate a feeding response. Juvenile salmonids in aquariums, for example, respond when small quantities of a given food extract are added to their water — but only if they've had experience with that particular food. Food selectivity may also depend on whether or not the food items are alive. Trout accustomed to one type of nonliving food, such as commercially prepared pellets, usually show a distinct preference for what they're used to if presented with an array of nonliving foods. But if trained to eat a certain form of living prey, trout don't always show preference for it when given a choice between that prey and a novel prey item that's also alive. On the other hand, trout on a feeding spree can be agonizingly selective, and the trout in some waters are very selective virtually all of the time.

Most animals are less selective when their hunger level is high, but there is evidence that the opposite is true for trout. According to the results of experiments, trout are more prone to consume novel foods during the second half of a feeding session than during the first half. But as a point of satiation is approached, they tend to "handle" their food more, frequently taking it into their mouths and rejecting it several times before finally swallowing it.

The feeding rate may be influenced both by the size and by the density of the prey. When laboratory rainbows were offered an abundance of amphipods (scuds) of several sizes, the trout assumed a searching position a few inches above and at an angle facing the bottom. But when the prey density was low and the fish were making fewer than 3.5 captures per minute on the average, the bottom-oriented search changed abruptly to more or less undirected swimming. When a choice of prey size was available, the rainbows also fed more heavily on larger amphipods, possibly because the larger ones attracted them from a greater distance, thereby increasing the rate of discovery. Table 6.1 shows the relationship between prey size and reactive distance (the distance from which trout were attracted) in these experiments.

Table 6.1. The relationship between prey size and the reactive distance of feeding trout

Prey Length (mm)	Mean Reactive Distance (mm)
4	180
5	220
6	280
7	280
9	350

SOURCE: Based on D. M. Ware, "Predation by Rainbow Trout *[Salmo gairdneri]*: The Influence of Hunger, Prey Density and Prey Size." *Journal of the Fisheries Research Board of Canada* 29(8), 1972, 1193-1201.

Food Color Choice

Evidence indicates that trout perceive color and are able to make food choices based on that perception. In one group of experiments, rainbow trout were allowed to feed on trout eggs dyed various colors. Different combinations of two colors were offered at a time. With natural lighting (330-380 foot candles) and a pale greenish blue background, the colors chosen (in order of preference) were blue, red, black, orange, brown, yellow, and green. Certain color combinations — yellow-black, yellow-blue, and red-orange — stimulated high consumption by the trout, while other combinations — yellow-orange and red-green — led to low consumption. Some colors elicited high consumption rates for eggs of other colors. Yellow had the greatest such effect and was followed by green, brown, orange, black, blue, and red.

Four food colors, in various combinations, were also presented to the fish against the greenish blue background, at reduced light intensities — anywhere from 0.1 to 1.2 foot candles. At these light levels, the color choices were quite different — in order of preference, yellow, red, blue, and black.

In experiments involving variations in background color, troughs were colored blue, red, black, or yellow, in shades approximating as closely as possible those of the eggs similarly colored. Although background color did influence the choice of food items, the results for different backgrounds varied. Except for the blue background, the consumption of eggs of the same color as the background was low. With a blue background, more blue eggs were consumed than eggs of any other color; with a red background, yellow eggs were most often eaten; with a yellow background, red eggs were preferred; and with a black background, red eggs were the first choice, closely followed by yellow eggs. The general conclusion suggested by these experiments is that the contrast of food color with background color is an important factor controlling the trout's choice of food; the blue egg-blue background correlation shows an exception to the usual behavior.

These experiments, although conducted under lab conditions and without any attempt to simulate a natural setting, demonstrate that color preference in food is influenced by the colors of nearby objects, by the general background color, and by the amount of ambient light available. That in itself should provide plenty of food for thought for anglers. But the results obtained from one group of experimental fish don't justify making broad generalizations about other salmonids. Different species, different strains of rainbows, and dissimilar environmental conditions might well have yielded a wide variety of results. And it's probable that previous experience would also have a bearing on the preferences of fish. Nobody has suggested that all fish under all conditions prefer the same food colors; but that color can influence food choice in salmonids isn't in doubt.

Reactions to Cover and Light

Food and cover are the major needs of trout — the two things that a good station should provide. But even second-rate stations appear to yield adequate food supplies under normal conditions, so it's cover that gives a station its advantage. The greater the cover, the more completely a trout can be concealed while still able to view drifting prey. And, naturally, dominant individuals within hierarchies gravitate toward such advantageous places.

One battery of experiments involving brook, brown, and rainbow trout and their cover revealed some interesting behavioral differences among the species. Rainbows made less use of cover than the other two species, since they were more apt to depart periodically from their stations. If something happened to reduce the amount of cover at a station, they also showed less delay in leaving for some other spot. In other words, they exhibited a lower degree of attachment to a station than either browns or brookies. Brown trout, on the other hand, tended to stay put: they made the greatest use of cover and tended to depart from their stations less than the other two species. These results tie in well with reports that browns, to a greater extent than other salmonids, are inclined toward inactivity in light.

Visual acuity in salmonids appears to increase with age. Very young fish don't display much of a response at all to variations in light intensity. Perhaps the best generalization that can be made about mature salmonids is that they are repelled by strong light and attracted to dim light. Since they feed by sight, feeding declines when light is reduced to a critically low level. Nor will young fish school without adequate illumination. There also appears to be a general consensus that reduced light levels coincide with diminished aggression.

West Coast biologists have managed to guide migrating steelhead and Pacific salmon by using lights of varying intensities. Strings of bright lights placed above the surface deflect the fish if the water is clear; but dim light acts as an attractant in either clear or turbid waters.

Learning and Memory

That trout are able to learn is amply demonstrated by their territoriality, their feeding behavior, and other activities. A few studies have attempted to quantify their learning capacity. For the most part this has
been done by getting the fish to do a simple task in order to obtain a
reward, such as a measure of food, or to avoid a bad experience, such as
an electric shock.

The subjects of one series of experiments were young rainbow
trout in aquariums. Just below the water's surface a red-tipped trigger-
ing device was placed which, when hit, would release a few food
pellets into the water. Linked with the trigger was a recording device
that kept a tally of the frequency with which the trigger was hit. In each
aquarium the daily number of contacts with the trigger increased from
fewer than 50 on the first day to about 250 after 10 days, a level at
which it remained thereafter (Figure 6.9). The trout had learned to
associate the movement of the trigger with a food reward in a period of
about 10 days.

During the learning period there were changes in the manner in
which the fish approached the trigger and put it into motion. At first
they attacked it, sometimes trying to swallow it as though it were a
piece of food. By the end of the training period they had learned simply
to nudge it with their lips (Figure 6.10). Similarly, in the early stages of
learning trout approached the trigger from any direction; after training,
their approach was made from an angle and at a speed that allowed

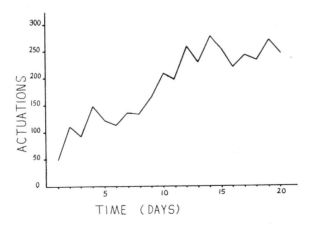

Figure 6.9. The learning period for young rainbow trout as expressed in number of actua-
tions of a feeding device per day for a population of 30 individuals. (After Adron, *et al.,*
1972.)

A.

B.

Figure 6.10. Young rainbows, such as the one in photograph A, tended to attack the trigger when first exposed to it (see text). After having learned that it was associated with a release of food they nudged it gently, as shown in photograph B. (Courtesy of Dr. J. W. Adron and the *Journal of Fish Biology*.)

them, by simply continuing their forward movement, to be at the spot where food pellets dropped into the aquarium.

Trout trained to the trigger were able to remember the task after months away from it. The experimentalists took some groups of fish that had been on the self-demand feeding program for 28 days, and for three months fed them by hand. At the end of this period, when the trout were returned to the demand feeders, they immediately took up their old self-feeding routine without requiring any retraining.

The rainbows also learned quickly to discriminate between two triggers. Some trout already trained to the self-demand system were transferred to a new tank having two triggers; only one of the two would release food. The trout learned to tell the difference between the triggers on their first day in the new tank, and from that time on the blank trigger was hit only about 5 times for every 100 hits on the food trigger.

In another set of experiments, using Atlantic salmon parr and yearling brook trout, the study fish were placed one at a time into an aquarium divided into two compartments by a partition. Each compartment had as a light source a 15-watt bulb, and an opening in the partition allowed fish to pass from one compartment to the other. Each fish was placed into a lighted compartment, while the other compartment was in darkness. The lights were then switched, so the fish suddenly found itself in darkness and the other compartment lit. Then electric shocks were delivered to the fish's compartment at intervals of two seconds until the fish reacted "correctly" by swimming through the opening into the lighted compartment, where it received no shock. At first, both the light charge and the shocks were presented together. After a number of such trials had taken place, however, the fish swam into the lighted compartment as soon as the light change was made, without waiting for a shock.

The light change itself, of course, didn't warrant hasty escape action, but it had become associated with the shocks. The experimentors in this case set the criterion for "learning" at 6 consecutive avoidances, and for both the salmon and the trout the average number of trials necessary for learning was between 25 and 30.

Navigation and Orientation

Some salmonids are among the most notable of migratory creatures; anadromous forms range out into oceans as far as 3,500 miles from the mouths of their home rivers. Pacific salmon from Alaskan rivers, for instance, have been found not far from Korea. The fact that such fish are able to find their way back not only to their home river, but also to their parent tributary stream, is linked primarily with their capacity for solar navigation and with their incredibly sensitive olfactory perception.

Salmonids can maintain an essentially straight course by using a moving body — the sun — as a reference point, a fact that clearly indicates internal compensation for the movement of the sun across the visible sky. As if this wasn't complex enough, the sun's rays are refracted when entering water (as discussed in Chapter 5), so from under water the sun appears to be in a different position at any given moment than it does to creatures above the surface. Yet the fish are able to make the additional compensation.

There may be another, as yet unexplained, method used by fish for navigation and orientation. Young sockeye salmon migrating from lakes toward the sea utilize sunlight when skies are clear, but as cloud cover begins to build up, disorientation sets in. With complete cloud cover, however, the fish recover their orientation; of necessity, this must be attributed to noncelestial phenomena. And if some of the migrating sockeyes are removed from the lakes and held in indoor tanks, they position themselves just as their brethren do within the lake system, in a direction appropriate to the migration route. The term "x-orientation" is sometimes used for this unexplained ability.

When considering navigation in salmonids, a distinction is usually made between long-range navigation and that which occurs in home waters. Cues from the sun appear to be the chief means of direction-finding in large bodies of water, but experts now agree that once a river system is entered, salmonids rely on their olfactory sense to guide them to their parent streams.

The ability of salmonids to smell their surroundings is nothing short of astounding. It's been demonstrated that they can detect dissolved substances in concentrations as low as one part in 3,000,000,000,000,000,000. Among the unique characteristics of any stream basin are the mineral formations over which the water flows and the soil and vegetation types lining the banks. And because trace amounts of many of these inorganic and organic substances can be found dissolved in stream waters, there is a distinctness, an individual aroma, to a given stream that can be perceived by fish.

Before migrating, young salmonids imprint on odors peculiar to their natal streams. Imprinting is a rapid learning process that occurs at an early age, and which is commonly characterized by a strong attachment to an object or a set of conditions. When departing from the waters of their early life, young migratory salmonids carry the "memory" of the odors of their natal stream, and they retain this memory into adult life. That attachment to natal waters is a learned rather than a genetic feature can be demonstrated by removing eggs from nests and transplanting them into a different stream. Fish developing from the transplanted eggs imprint on — and ultimately return to — the new stream.

Although salmonids generally return to their parent stream to spawn, there are usually a few individuals that run to other streams. Such strays occasionally show up in biologists' fish traps. The reported number of straying fish may range up to 15 percent or more of the total number of migrating fish in a given population, but some reports may not be valid since salmonids may ascend a stream for a considerable distance before turning and going back downstream. And if they happen to get caught in a trap, they'll be recorded as strays even though they might eventually have arrived at their parent stream.

It is generally agreed that odors of plant and mineral origin act as guides for homing salmonids, but there's also a possibility that substances given off by fish themselves may act as guides in some cases. Young Arctic char, for example, exhibit a preference for water containing odorants of char over water without such odors. And some biologists have been able to get varying responses in char to odors from four different char populations. Furthermore, experiments in Norway show that char that have never had a chance to imprint on a home stream (having been raised in laboratories) still tend to run up rivers populated by char of related stocks. So there's a possibility that the presence of fish can condition water in such a way that returning fish recognize the stream as the habitat of "relatives." There is evidence that external mucus is the source of these attractants.

Sounds and Sound Perception

During a series of experiments on the cutthroat trout of Yellowstone Lake (Wyoming), sounds emitted by the trout were recorded and analyzed. Three distinct sounds were distinguished. "Thumps" occurred singly or in a rapid series when a trout gave a sudden flip of the tail and changed direction, apparently as a result of being startled. This happened, for instance, when gulls or ospreys flew overhead. When one trout gave forth with a thump, nearby trout darted away, so the sound may have had a warning value. The actual source of the sound isn't known for sure, but it may be caused by the sudden contraction of muscles.

When a trout had surfaced and then returned to its position, it often gave a "squawk." Sometimes the sound was emitted only after several seconds had elapsed following the return of the fish. The investigator suggested that it was caused by the passage of air from the duct leading from the swim bladder, since when diving into deeper water, fish often expel air in such a way. Infrequently, a squawk would be followed by a "squeak" of low intensity.

Salmonids are reported to hear tones ranging from 10 to between 500 and 1,000 cycles per second (the greater the frequency, the higher the pitch of the sound produced). Trout thumps were recorded as being 100-200 cps and squawks as 600-850 cps, so the fish probably hear them. But the squeaks are so high-pitched (1200-1500 cps) as to be out of their estimated hearing range.

Displacement Activity

A displacement activity is an activity performed out of context. In other words, it's an act that seems totally inappropriate to the situation. Prey-shaking, for example, that violent side-to-side motion of the head that salmonids often perform after having captured large prey, is sometimes performed by fish that aren't even feeding. This has been classified as a displacement activity. Spawning Arctic char, apparently with a kind of aggressive fervor, sometimes pick up a rock or a mouthful of sand and spit it out. And young Atlantic salmon defending territories have been described as becoming "irritated" when they caught glimpses of neighboring fish, and reacting by tearing rooted algae from the bottom, shaking it, and spitting it out.

In the interpretation of animal behavior patterns, anthropomorphism (the use of human behavior as a model for interpretations) is very much frowned upon. It's acceptable to say that a salmon is performing a displaced act by throwing some algae around, because such a statement doesn't offend the definition for displacement activity. But to state flatly that the fish is experiencing irritation is to tread on thin ice, since the emotional state of the creature just isn't known, nor can it be with the tools and techniques presently at hand. So behaviorists usually bend over backward to avoid anthropomorphic statements. Still, they do crop up from time to time.

Certain areas in any given stretch of water, by the very nature of what that water offers in the way of drift patterns and cover, attract hierarchies of trout. Even if a local population was to become temporarily depleted, the desirable aspects of the area that attracted fish in the first place would certainly attract other fish later on. A good spot, in other words, should remain a good spot — barring geologic catastrophy or the bulldozer. And such a spot, once found, should be a source of fish year after year.

Territories within the area are established along major drift patterns, and the best stations, which attract the biggest trout, are close to superior cover. Again, the desirability of a prime station is a static thing, and as soon as a fish is caught from it, another will probably move in before too long. If one trout perceives it as a good location, others will too.

As trout settle into an area they become accustomed to feeding on the prey locally prevalent. It's here that the angler using artificials has to be especially attentive. Because his flies and lures lack the scents of things edible, his success is going to depend primarily on visual deception.

After spending enough time on a river, one gets to know some of the rocks and eddies and undercuts that mark first-rate stations. A feel develops for the rhythm of feeding patterns. And watching hatches, turning stones, and occasionally going through stomachs turns up evidence of what foods fish are likely to prefer. Knowing how trout are liable to act in given situations can be valuable information for anyone stalking these fish. Getting to know a stream translates to a large degree into learning something of the behavior of its residents.

7.
Reproductive Behavior

In the realm of behavior, the hereditary co-ordinations or instinct movements are independent building stones. As unchangeable in their form as the hardest skeletal component, each one cracks its own whip over the organism as a whole. —Konrad Lorenz, 1963

Migration

Salmonids usually spawn in cold, well-oxygenated streams with gravel bottoms — the kind of areas associated with the headwaters of river systems. So when fish begin to get the spawning urge, there's an upstream migration of anywhere from a couple of hundred feet to well over a thousand miles. Chinook salmon are real distance champions, sometimes running as far as 2,000 miles up the Yukon River to their breeding grounds. During spawning runs fish may accomplish heroic feats to get by obstacles such as falls, occasionally making leaps amounting to five or six times their body length. Fatal injuries aren't uncommon if fish are swept back onto rocks. Upstream migrations are the norm, but some species (e.g., golden trout and landlocked salmon) often run down the outlet of a lake to their spawning areas.

The time of year when a given population spawns is determined primarily by heredity, though factors external to the fish may have modifying effects. Most of the more familiar species (brookies, browns, Dolly Vardens, and others) are fall spawners, but some (cutthroats, for example) are usually spring spawners. Considerable variations in timing may exist within a species. Among rainbows, some runs take place in the spring and others in autumn; Pacific salmon are seen spawning from March to December.

The control and timing of migration and spawning are regulated by the nervous system and the endocrine system (the latter made up of glands that produce hormones and release them into the bloodstream). The nervous and endocrine systems, in turn, are influenced by seasonal cycles and their variations in day-length, temperature, and precipitation, and as a result the time of migration for any given population can generally be predicted with reasonable accuracy. But year to year variations occur, indicating that the effects of variable factors such as barometric pressure and precipitation are superimposed upon that most obvious of factors that can be relied upon, day-length.

Although parent stream homing, or natal homing as it's sometimes called, is the general rule in salmonids, there is often some interchange of individuals between river systems, with crossbreeding between populations being an inevitable result. Such interchanging may be more prevalent in some populations than in others. But even though some interchange takes place, the practice of homing to natal waters allows each population to maintain a certain degree of genetic integrity, since there tends to be a low rate of gene transfer between populations. Each population, then, tends to be especially well adapted to the unique complex of conditions it encounters in its environment. As an established population makes its migration, it is able to respond to the various demands made at each stage. The precise behavior patterns that characterize such a population are the result of natural selection, so homing, because it favors breeding within the population, insures maintenance of the appropriate behavior patterns.

Because salmonids depend upon proper responses to given stimuli, it isn't surprising that conditions inappropriate for a certain migrating population can severely reduce spawning success and possibly prevent it entirely. When a new run of salmon is becoming established, for example, the percentage of fish returning to the spawning area is often quite poor at first. By contrast, if a calamity depletes an established population, the few survivors, being genetically adapted to the local environment, may rebuild the population very quickly.

Once fish have congregated to make an upstream migration, numerous factors may act to favor the run or to impede it. For anadromous salmonids, the flow rate of the current appears to be a major controlling factor, if not the most important one. It's been observed that freshets often produce an increase in the numbers of migrating fish. In rivers where flow can be regulated, releases of water are sometimes used to stimulate spawning runs.

The effects of flow rate can be modified by many things. The effectiveness of a freshet to stimulate a run may be enhanced by various combinations of wind and tide — for example, when they act to keep streamwater close to a coastline as they often do. Both unseasonably high and low temperature readings may impede migration. And one study (using rainbow trout) concluded that falling atmospheric pressure favors migration, rising pressure inhibits it, and that changing pressure rather than absolute pressure was the important factor.

Although salmonids require adequate light for contending with obstacles, they often do most of their migrating under cover of darkness, a habit that has been associated with predator avoidance. People who try to stimulate migration by releasing water from upstream impoundments often time such releases to allow the increased flow to reach the river mouth at dusk. On the other hand, there are enough reports of major migration activities during daylight hours to infer that a preference for darkness shouldn't be thought of as a hard and fast rule. Most daytime runs, though, do take place in turbid water, which by its very nature offers a visual shield.

The physical factors bearing in some way on salmonid runs are numerous enough and often so interdependent that they ought to be considered together rather than as isolated entities. Back in the 1950s, for instance, it was reported that migrating sockeyes being studied moved upstream under conditions of rising temperature and pH and falling oxygen and carbon dioxide concentrations. But the mechanism ultimately responsible for the proper synchronization of these factors was apparently the local light intensity cycle, which had a bearing not only on temperature but also on plant photosynthesis, which in turn affected the levels of dissolved gases and pH.

Most studies dealing with migration in salmonids have concentrated on anadromous fish in the act of entering fresh water from the sea. But even the available information about this subject is fairly sparse and sometimes conflicting. Perhaps it is best simply to draw attention to the uniqueness of each river system, and to the fact that native populations have been molded by evolution to be finely in tune with their respective environments.

Spawning Behavior

Salmonids may arrive on their spawning grounds days or even weeks before actual spawning takes place. Females soon begin to explore the gravel bottom to find sites for suitable beds and to perform some digging motions. Digging, more often referred to as cutting, is a complex of muscular contractions employed to displace gravel, and is virtually universal among the salmonids. When cutting, a fish turns onto her side and, facing upstream, alternately bends and straightens her body so that the fanned-out caudal fin flaps vertically (Figure 7.1). The curve to her body places the tail region rather than the head closer to the substrate. Although it appears that strong physical contact is made with the gravel (especially to someone looking down from above the surface), it is actually pressure change caused by the vertical motion of the tail that shifts the gravel; and although the pressure increase caused by a downstroke may loosen material, it's suction from the upstroke that's responsible for actual displacement. The fish may use its right and left sides with equal frequency. A single cut might vary in intensity from a few weak movements to as many as a dozen vigorous movements at a rate of three or four per second. The process is surprisingly effective — foot-long fish are able to move rocks larger than an inch and a half in diameter.

In the earliest stages of bed preparation the cuts made by females may be relatively feeble, and are apparently directed at random rather than toward a specific site. Often the fish tend to work their way upstream. Males don't show much interest at this time.

If the process continues normally, suitable bed material is found and cuts become more vigorous and of longer duration. After making a cut, which drives her a short distance upstream, a fish often returns im-

Figure 7.1. A female brown in the act of cutting. (Courtesy of J. N. Ball.)

mediately or following a short delay and feels the developing bed with her anal fin, and sometimes with her pelvic fins as well. To do this she might drift down to the area of the cut, or swim downstream and approach the bed from below. The bed is also comprehended visually: cutting fish sometimes look down at a developing bed (indicated by eye movement and a tilting of the head) before making a new cut. In any case, it's when vigorous cutting takes place that males show an interest.

Not much has been written about the criteria used by salmonids in selecting mates, but selection does appear to be influenced by general fitness and aggressiveness, by the degree of development of secondary sex characteristics (such as the intensity of spawning coloration and elongation of the jaws), and by readiness to spawn at a given time. Understandably, small males usually aren't as successful as big ones in defending beds, so they're more apt to be found alone or in the groups (satellite males) sometimes seen downstream of spawning pairs.

According to most reports, a male that has successfully paired up with a cutting female usually positions himself just downstream and to one side of the female. Between cuts he might draw alongside her and quiver, an act that has come to be known as courting.

When excavation is in full swing, cuts may come in such rapid succession that a depression soon begins to form. Between cuts the female feels the depression frequently, especially with her anal fin; apparently this is a means of gathering information about the condition of the substrate. Sometimes cutting activity is as great at night as it is during the day.

As bed preparation proceeds, the dominant male (a male that has paired with a female and successfully defends his standing and the developing bed) courts with increasing intensity, sometimes quivering several times between each cut. Quivering, though occasionally seen in females and nondominant males, is especially associated with courting by the dominant male, so it may have a stimulatory function, at least when directed toward a female. Now and then, however, quivering is directed toward intruding males as an apparent threat, and males have even been seen quivering at inanimate objects, so there might be a variety of functions involved. It has also been suggested that it represents a low-intensity form of the spawning act.

A dominant male can be a busy creature, because there are always other males waiting in the wings to replace him. The satellite males, normally a short distance downstream of a spawning pair, are strung out in such a way that the most dominant of their number is farthest upstream. When the spawning male on the bed departs, the number one satellite male immediately goes in and takes over the defense of the bed and other duties until the dominant male returns. As it happens, bedding females chase away intruders approaching from upstream, but not those coming up from below. No doubt there's a connection between this behavior and the downstream positioning of satellite males. A dominant male sometimes tries to hold more than a single female, but naturally this compounds his problems and increases the risk of his losing a given female to a competitor.

The bed is round to oval in shape, and if it is oval the long axis is parallel to the current. In length, the bed may approximate that of the fish making it, or it may be up to three times as long as the fish. The depth of a foot-long bed might be two or three inches, with longer beds correspondingly deeper. In any event, the depth normally exceeds the greatest depth of the fish making it. On the downstream side of the bed a mound or "tail-spill" of displaced material piles up (Figure 7.2). The concavity of the bed itself, along with the tail-spill, creates eddies that tend to keep particles within the bed that might otherwise be swept away immediately. These factors also aid in the mixing of eggs and milt and in keeping the eggs within the bed until they can be covered.

The period required for completion of a bed might be anywhere from several hours to several days. In the final stages of preparation the female changes her cutting technique to one that employs the back of the body rather than the caudal fin (Figure 7.3), a modification that keeps her from being driven upstream where gravel could be dislodged and swept down into the nearly completed bed. She also begins to position herself closer to the bottom between cuts, sometimes forcing her erect anal fin into a crevice between two stones. During this crouch her body arches so that her head is elevated and the area of her vent is snug within the bed. Of course, a substrate that allows the anal fin to be hid-

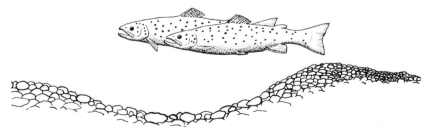

Figure 7.2. A pair of trout on a completed bed. The male is just below the female. Below his caudal fin is the tail-spill of the bed.

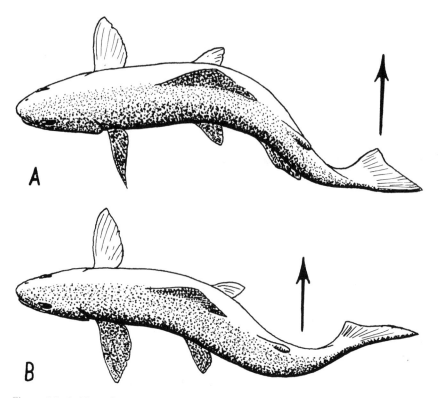

Figure 7.3. A. Normal cutting technique, in which the caudal fin is used.
B. Technique used in the later stages of bed construction, employing the posterior part of the body. (Modified from Jones and Ball, 1954.)

den also insures the deposition of eggs within a permeable, or "open," material — a condition necessary for egg survival.

Courting increases in intensity during this period, the male perhaps leaking small amounts of milt on occasion. Each time the female crouches the male darts alongside her and quivers, and if the bed is satisfactory to the fish, orgasm may occur. The female opens her mouth, and the male, now alongside her and quivering violently, opens his as well. The female then widens her gape to its fullest extent and goes into what appears to be a state of extreme muscular tension; at this time the eggs pass from her, most of them falling between the stones into the crevice where her anal fin is hidden. Simultaneously the quivering male, whose vent is in close proximity to that of the female, ejaculates into the bed. The milt explodes forth as a white cloud (Figure 7.4). The crouch and the open mouth of a ready female probably stimulate the male to dart in and ejaculate, but there is also evidence

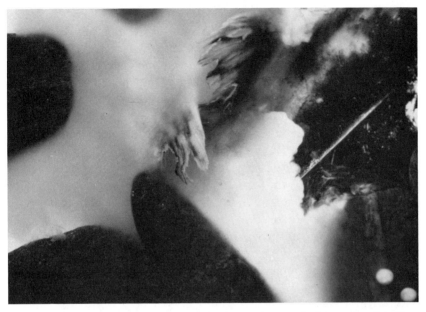

Figure 7.4. A ventral view of spawning pink salmon, photographed through a plate glass bottom. The fish are seen at the upper right. A cloud of milt fills the interstices between the stones of the bed. Two eggs may be seen in the lower right-hand corner. (Copyright National Geographic Society.)

that chemical signals or attractants are involved as well. The actual orgasm lasts no more than one or two seconds. After being ejaculated, sperm must fertilize eggs within half a minute or so for they soon become inactive.

The salmonid spawning act doesn't always come off like a well-oiled machine. According to most detailed reports, a number of incomplete acts may take place before eggs and milt are finally released. In such cases, the spawning act seems about to take place but terminates before really getting started. Milt is sometimes shed in volumes that appear to constitute full loads. In one reported case a male was seen to ejaculate, then to swim upward and away from the female; some seconds later she shed her eggs in what was described as a "delayed orgasm." How the investigators determined that her orgasm was delayed, rather than that his ejaculation was premature, wasn't made clear.

Immediately following the spawning act the female hurries to the upstream side of the bed, and cuts vigorously, so that gravel is swept down into the bed and covers the eggs. During postspawning activity cuts are typically made more frequently than they were during bed construction, apparently to cover the eggs as quickly as possible. Predation, current, and the rapid loss of the adhesive qualities of the eggs make early covering essential. Between cuts the female may dart back to the nest for a short stay. By the time covering has been completed there's usually a bulge in the bottom to show the location of the former bed. The structure is now known as a redd, though some biologists don't make this distinction and apply the term to a bed in any stage of completion. Both salmonid sexes normally participate in several mating acts with various partners before becoming spent.

In most cases the defense of redds is a function of females, since males normally desert the redd during the early stages of egg covering. Females sometimes hang around for days or even weeks driving intruders away from redd areas. But there are exceptions, because in some populations females depart from the spawning area before males do — another example, perhaps, of the variation that can exist among different breeding populations.

Most of the chars — brookies, Dolly Vardens, and Arctic char — have a different technique for covering their eggs. Instead of cutting they simply sweep the area around the bed with the tail, or use the caudal and anal fins to push bottom material over the eggs. Compared with the covering-by-cutting process these methods are not efficient, but the charts have persisted, so their methods have served them at least adequately.

In streams, females usually go a short distance upstream of a redd to begin cutting another bed, but sometimes they move into a different area of the stream.

On occasion different species (e.g., brook trout and browns) may be found breeding in the same area at the same time. Although fish breed almost exclusively with members of their own species, hybrids are occasionally found in nature. In western states, where rainbows and cutthroats cohabit, hybrids are common.

One of the best and most detailed studies of salmonid reproductive behavior (often cited by other writers) is a classic that was published by J. W. Jones and J. N. Ball in 1954. These biologists analyzed slow motion movies of mating brown trout and Atlantic salmon in running water, and their diagrammatic organization of the events that occur during spawning has served as a model for subsequent students (Figure 7.5).

		Male	Female
Reproductive Instinct	Courting and Fighting	pushing tail flicking quivering chasing biting	pushing tail flicking quivering (trout, rarely) chasing biting
	Building	defence against intrusion	cutting (all stages) feeling crouching exploratory quivers
	Mating	darting movements quivering mouth opening orgasm	final crouching mouth opening muscle tension orgasm
	Care of Offspring	trout—stands by nest salmon—often moves away	covering up of eggs defensive circling

Figure 7.5. A hierarchical classification of aspects of salmonid reproductive behavior. (After Jones and Ball, 1954.)

Spawning Behavior in Arctic Char and Lake Trout

At about the same time that Jones and Ball were doing their work, E. Fabricius and K. J. Gustafson were doing classic studies of salmonid reproduction in still water. Their study fish was the Arctic char, a species that may spawn naturally either in streams or over rocky lake bottoms.

In still water male char defend territories, and pair formation takes place when a female swims into a territory. The male, strangely enough, attacks the female and for his trouble he's counterattacked. Attacks by the male gradually give way to courting behavior, and this in turn prompts the female to begin cutting. During spawning itself the female swims in a circle, dropping into the bed each time she passes over it. The male swims in a larger circle, timing his arrivals at the bed to coincide with those of the female and gliding alongside her at each pass (Figure 7.6). Courting and spawning then proceed as they do in salmonids in running water. The spawning acts occur in groups of one to five, with a few minutes between acts. And whereas most salmonids immediately cover their eggs after each batch has been released, Arctic char living in still water wait until all matings in a group have been accomplished. Then, in typical char fashion, the female, maintaining an upright posture, goes through an undulating, sweeping motion. But

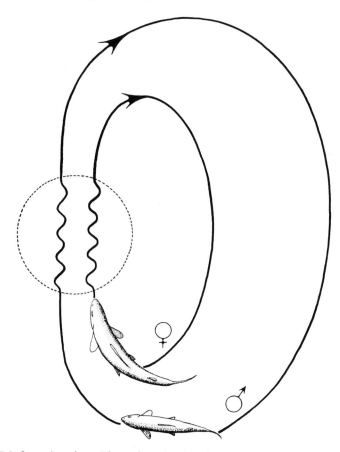

Figure 7.6. Spawning chars. The male swims in a large circle which encompasses the smaller one described by the female, and his arrivals at the bed (depicted by the circle with the broken outline) are timed to coincide with those of the female. The undulating lines within the bed are indicative of courting and spawning acts. (Modified from Eric Fabricius, *Aquarium Observations on the Spawning Behaviour of the Char, Salvelinus alpinus*. Institute of Freshwater Research, Report no. 34, Drottningholm, 1953, pp. 14-18.)

even though she might keep this up for as much as three-quarters of an hour, it doesn't do much more than roll the eggs about. Survival of the eggs seems to depend pretty heavily on bottom type — on their being wafted into crevices between stones. When a female char in still water begins a subsequent bed it's usually next to the one just completed, so bottom material does sometimes get kicked over exposed eggs. All of the beds she makes — as many as eight per female have been seen — tend to be close to one another and in a row.

Lake trout are unique among salmonids, since they usually spawn in lakes along rock- and boulder-strewn shorelines, displaying a lack of attachment to localized beds. Males arrive on the spawning grounds before females, and cruise about fanning the bottom to clean a substantial area of any sediment that might be there. Rocks get moved in this way too, and a lot of the fish become abraded from their activities. When females arrive, courting and spawning begin, taking place more or less at random on the cleaned area. Fighting is rare.

In courting lake trout it's typical for either one or two males to approach a female and, while quivering, to press their vents to her sides. But such activity isn't confined to just two or three individuals at a time: regular piscine orgies have been seen involving as many as 10 fish, all pressed together and quivering. The eggs are simply broadcast, and the fish make no attempt to cover them. Many of them gain protection by falling into crevices.

Combat During Spawning

Peace rarely reigns on spawning grounds. Attacks and counterattacks are frequent, and fights can be long and heated. Many conflicts involve a dominant male and an intruder, male or female. Satellite males are strung out below a spawning pair, each dominant over others in the group that are yet farther downstream, and an attempt by any individual to move forward will often evoke aggression from the fish just ahead. Occasionally, a dominant male gets a bite from a cutting female. There are no reports of a subordinate male actually attacking a dominant male stationed on a bed, though infrequent instances of half-hearted snaps being made at his tail have been observed. Male sockeyes, probably because of their well-developed kypes, sometimes get their teeth caught on adversaries, and the two fish may drift downstream some distance before getting free of one another.

Many biologists have reported fighting of a formal nature in spawning salmonids. Jones and Ball recorded bouts of perhaps 10 minutes duration, following a distinct pattern, among brown trout of about equal size. A female when cutting a bed would not allow other fish to lie ahead of her. When an intruder of either sex moved upstream to position itself parallel to the resident, with its snout only a few inches in front of the resident's, the resident would move ahead until her eye was about level with the intruder's snout. As these maneuvers were repeated, the two fish progressed upstream. The upstream movement was interrupted when the challenger cut in front of the resident, the resident charged the challenger, and the challenger evaded a charge by quickly twisting about and coming up parallel to the resident once more (Figure 7.7). The process was repeated until the resident grabbed the intruder by the tail and dragged the unresisting fish backward downstream a number of feet. Then more forward progressions and flanking maneuvers ensued, until at last the conflict ended.

Dominance between spawning males is sometimes determined by formal fights. Brown trout may position themselves one behind the other; then one fish — either one — attacks and grasps the other, which before long generally wrenches itself free. Tandem positions are taken again, and the cycle is repeated. The winner is the trout making the more frequent and vigorous attacks. Shorter fights take place in which the male combatants swim in a circle and try to grab one another's tails; these usually ending with one fish simply swimming away. Similar fights take place between Atlantic salmon males.

Male rainbows on spawning grounds have been seen to swim upstream side by side, when one of them then drops downstream, gathers momentum, and rams the other as hard as possible in the middle of the body. The trout first attacked then takes a turn in ramming the other. And oddly enough, even though 30-inch fish have been seen

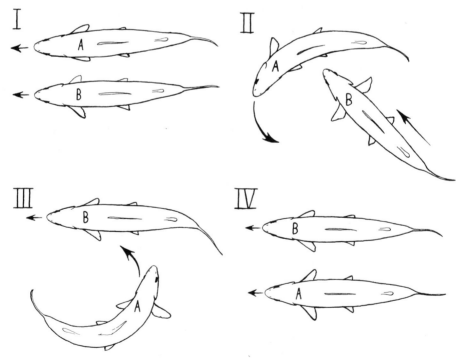

Figure 7.7. Formal combat between female salmonids (see text). In part II of the sequence, fish B is launching an attack, which is evaded by fish A. (Modified from Jones and Ball, 1954.)

engaged in such contests — a lot of force would be behind those punches — the attacks are accepted without apparent fear. How such fights are terminated and how a winner is determined have not been described.

Nonviolent techniques appear especially successful in removing intruders from beds. Resident Atlantic salmon sometimes run upstream a short distance and then drift down toward their beds in a tail-first approach, or with the body at an angle to the current; sometimes the intruder is given a little sideways flick of the tail. No violence, but it always seems to do the trick in getting rid of trespassers.

The Fate of Eggs

When eggs are passed into the bed they're slightly adhesive, a quality they quickly lose as water-hardening takes place. Hardening occurs when water enters minute pores in the outer shell, filling the space between the shell and the yolk membrane, and causing the egg to swell by perhaps 20 to 30 percent. As an egg swells, its surface becomes taut and elastic.

The micropyle, that hole through which the sperm enters, is at its greatest diameter when the egg is passed, but as hardening proceeds its diameter decreases until the hole closes, making fertilization impossible. This means that an egg is most capable of being fertilized immediately upon leaving the body, and that this capability starts to decline immediately. It's generally understood that eggs have lost all viability three minutes after being passed.

Because orgasm is generally simultaneous, and because there are eddies of current within the depression of the bed, eggs and sperm are quickly mixed. By most accounts, well over 90 percent of all eggs become fertilized before the micropyle closes, but figures as low as 27 percent have been reported. In any event, since the female quickly busies herself with covering the eggs, they're soon secure beneath a layer of gravel.

Eggs that are washed out of the bed before being covered are usually quickly eaten, because natural waters teem with creatures that feed on them, including salmonids themselves. When, on occasion, a female decides to cut on a recently completed redd, the eggs are exposed to predation. And even spent females may continue to cut for awhile if there's enough of their reproductive drive intact.

Egg Development and Hatching

As soon as an egg is fertilized development begins. Internally, the egg divides into two cells, then the two divide into four, the four into eight, and so on, until in time there are legions of cells from which a tiny salmonid body begins to form (Figure 7.8).

The rate at which salmonid eggs develop depends upon water temperature. One old rule of thumb for brook trout holds that the incubation period (the time from fertilization to hatching) is 50 days at a temperature of 50° F (10° C) and that hatching will occur 5 days sooner for each added Fahrenheit degree, or 5 days later for each degree of heat removed. Actually such rules are shaky at best, because incubation periods at a given water temperature can vary by as much as 6 days among fish of the same species. As a matter of fact, some sources give the incubation period for brookies as 44 or 45 days at 50° F. In general — and at 50° F — rainbows have a relatively short incubation period of about a month. Lake trout have a relatively long one, 50 days or so. Other common salmonids tend to be somewhere in between. Eggs don't incubate well at over 55° F (12.8° C), and at very low temperatures incubation becomes extremely lengthy and is said to result in weakened fry. At 35° F (1.7° C), for example, eggs of most species take more than four months to hatch — if they hatch at all.

During the first few days after fertilization the eggs are tough enough to stand moderate jarring without damage. But they then enter a sensitive period in which even slight jostling is likely to damage the developing membranes, and to result in death. This period lasts until

Figure 7.8. A developing salmonid egg in which an embryo may be seen.

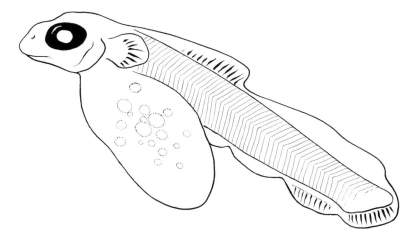

Figure 7.9. A newly hatched salmonid with attached yolk sac.

the eyes of the embryo are visible, perhaps a third of the way through development. By that time the eggs, referred to as eyed, are highly resistant to shock.

As development proceeds the oxygen requirement of the eggs increases. This is what makes the openness of a redd — the adequate spacing between pieces of gravel — so important, because oxygen-laden water can percolate through the spaces and reach the eggs. Openness also helps to keep the eggs clean of silt that might otherwise smother them.

Hatching takes place right in the gravel when the outer membrane ruptures. The newly hatched salmonids are not able to feed or even to move about, but during development within the egg layers of tissue grew around the egg yolk to form a yolk sac that will remain as a pendulous attachment for some weeks after hatching (Figure 7.9); and from the yolk in the sac the infant fry will draw nutrient material until they are able to feed on their own. After several weeks, the fish have grown enough to work their way up through the gravel to open water. There they establish feeding territories, if they've hatched in running water. If they find themselves in still waters, they tend to school, with the result that they will move about, feeding without fixation to a territory.

The early life of salmonids is a major hurdle. Only a relative few of the hardiest individuals will overcome the combined pressures of predation, relentless competition, and the physical abuses heaped on them by a perilous environment. In most cases, fewer than 1 percent of newly hatched fry will survive the first year. We have already seen how fry establish territories within mosaics and, then, after forsaking the mosaics, become parts of social hierarchies. The fate of populations and the production of trout flesh within them — so important to anglers and fisheries biologists alike — is dealt with in the final chapter.

8.
Trout Populations and Trout Production

I suggest that the earth's biota is our single most important resource.
—GEORGE M. WOODWELL, 1974

Ecosystems

A community, in the sense used by biologists, is a complex of populations of organisms (plants, animals, bacteria — everything alive) that inhabit a definable area. And if, in addition to the living stuff in an area, the legions of nonliving factors such as light, temperature, and chemical makeup are considered, one speaks of an ecosystem. An ecosystem is a more or less enclosed unit with its living and nonliving parts. Typical examples might include a pond, a coral reef, or an isolated valley. Each would be characterized by fairly distinct flora and fauna, as well as by physical and chemical properties, setting it apart to a greater or lesser degree from surrounding ecosystems.

In reality, an ecosystem is only partly enclosed because there's always going to be some gain and loss of materials — some exchange with surrounding areas. Along a trout stream, for instance, there would be plenty of terrestrial creatures, leaf litter, and the like falling into the water. Flying aquatic insects being picked off by swallows would represent a material loss for the stream ecosystem.

Organisms in an ecosystem — members of the community — can be separated into three broad categories, depending on how they function in the funneling of matter and energy through the ecosystem. Producers, most of which are plants, are able to manufacture their own food by using light energy from the sun and raw materials that are part of the nonliving environment (the process called photosynthesis). Only producers can make food absolutely from scratch, so everything else in a community depends on them.

Most of the other species in a community are consumers of various sorts — animals incapable of making their own food and re-

171

quired to consume others in order to get the materials and energy required to survive in the world. Those that are herbivorous (feed directly on plants) are a community's primary consumers. Carnivores are
referred to as secondary consumers if they feed on primary consumers,
as tertiary consumers if they eat secondary consumers, and so on.

In a typical community some species are capable of using a broad
range of food items — of feeding at various levels in the food chain. This
means that they can act simultaneously as primary and secondary consumers, for example, or perhaps as secondary and tertiary consumers.
Salmonids are included among such creatures because they can feed on
a wide variety of animals. In any ecosystem in which they are found,
salmonids qualify as secondary consumers or higher, depending on the
food habits of the creatures they eat.

Finally, in addition to producers and consumers, a community
has its decomposers, chiefly in the form of bacteria and fungi. Decomposers chemically break down waste organic matter, including the
bodies of dead organisms, and in so doing they receive nourishment
even as they return chemicals to the ecosystem. Basically, then, matter
in an ecosystem is continually recycled: incorporated into living tissue
by producers, it is passed up through a chain of consumers and then
returned to the ecosystem in nonliving form by decomposers;
whereupon it's available to new generations of producers.

A small (and strictly hypothetical) trout pond containing a limited
number of species would make an ideal model ecosystem. The algae in
it use sunlight to make plant sugars, the food they then use for growth,
self-maintenance and reproduction. Within the pond there's also a
population of herbivorous amphipods whose food source is the algae;
the amphipods are therefore primary consumers, and algae, along with
excess food they've manufactured and stored within themselves, go
toward the formation of amphipod tissue. The production of amphipods in this model ecosystem hinges upon the availability of algae
(there are a number of things that might limit a population, but it's con-
venient to think of food supply as the most important factor). Secondary consumers in the pond are represented by a population of brook
trout, which prey upon the amphipods. We now have what is known as
a food chain (algae-amphipods-trout). But such relationships within an
ecosystem can be more precisely represented by a food pyramid
(Figures 8.1 and 8.2), showing producers at its broad base and terminal
consumers (the trout in this case) at the top.

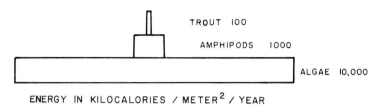

ENERGY IN KILOCALORIES / METER^2 / YEAR

Figure 8.1. A food pyramid expressing energy in kilocalories (a unit expressing the energy content of plant or animal tissue) for the trophic levels of a hypothetical ecosystem.

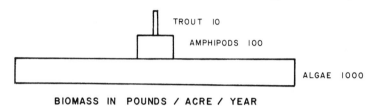

BIOMASS IN POUNDS / ACRE / YEAR

Figure 8.2. A food pyramid expressing biomass (total weight of tissue) for the trophic levels of a hypothetical ecosystem.

Food Pyramids

Food pyramids are simple diagrams that give a picture of the materials or energy flowing through an ecosystem. They can be set up to show the amount of plant and animal tissue being produced over a given time period (this is called productivity), or they can show the amount of energy for a given area over a given span of time.

The pyramid in Figure 8.1 shows the flow of energy in the hypothetical pond. It's probable that less than 1 percent of the solar energy falling on the water's surface actually gets used by producers, and in most cases, anywhere from 5 to 15 percent of the energy in any given level of the food pyramid gets transferred to the next level. The amount of energy found in any plant or animal tissue, which can be measured fairly easily by burning a sample of it in a calorimeter, is usually expressed in kilocalories. For each level in the pyramid in Figure 8.1, the round figure of 10 percent transfer efficiency was assumed. This means that of the energy tied up in any one level, only a tenth of it will make it to the next level up.

The pyramid in Figure 8.2 shows the total biomass produced annually within the hypothetical pond. Biomass, as the word suggests, simply refers to an amount (weight) of tissue. As was the case for the energy pyramid, a 10 percent efficiency was assumed, so that the biomass within a given level of the pyramid is but one-tenth that of the biomass in the level directly below. This pyramid shows that an acre of the model ecosystem produces half a ton of algae in a year, but only one hundred pounds of amphipods and ten pounds of brook trout. And if trout-eating otters were added to the pond — they would be tertiary consumers — the yield would be about one pound of otter tissue per year for each acre.

Just why are so little matter and energy transferred from one level of the food pyramid to another? For one thing, of all the tissue represented in any given level of the food chain and available to the next level, not every last bit will be eaten (some of the amphipods, for instance, will succumb to old age rather than to predation by trout). Of the tissue that is eaten, some won't be assimilated — some of the skeletal parts perhaps; and of that which is assimilated some will be used for respiration, some for reproduction, and some for growth. Only tissue that is actually used for growth, for the production of new tissue, will become available to still another level in the food chain.[1] So 10 percent efficiencies really aren't that bad.

Because a given level in a food chain (or pyramid) will always yield a lot less tissue than the level below it, more efficient use of an ecosystem can be made by our harvesting at lower levels. In the hypothetical trout pond, we'd harvest more in terms of sheer weight (by tenfold) in the unlikely event that we could become content to eat amphipods rather than trout. In some densely populated countries where protein is in short supply, strictly herbivorous fish are cultured which, because they feed directly on producers, yield a lot more fish flesh per acre than salmonids ever could. On the other hand, everything else being equal, trout yield more than some other game fish such as northern pike, because trout are primarily insect eaters, while pike feed most heavily on fish and are therefore higher in the food chain. Harvesting or eating high up on the food chain is really a kind of luxury.

All of this means that there's no way to get an increased, sustained yield from a piece of trout water without creating conditions that will increase yield at the producer level. If a greater yield is wanted at the top of the food pyramid, the base must be broadened. This principle has been put into practice in some Wisconsin streams where heavy vegetation along the banks had been preventing adequate amounts of

1. There is also a fundamental physical law, the Second Law of Thermodynamics, which states that in no chemical reaction, including any taking place in the body, is there a perfectly efficient transfer of energy. Some of the energy will dissipate into the surrounding environment.

sunlight from entering the water. The removal of some of the terrestrial vegetation led to increases in aquatic producer organisms, and in time trout production rose accordingly.

It's of more than passing interest that some pollutants, in proceeding through a food chain from one level to another, become increasingly concentrated in each successive level of the chain. This is known as biological magnification. DDT, for example, becomes incorporated into the tissues of organisms in the lower levels of food chains, and ever-increasing concentrations can be detected in the consecutive levels leading up to top level consumers, which have the highest concentrations. Some of the larger coho salmon and brown trout in Lake Michigan, which are top level consumers in food chains there, have been found to contain DDT in their fat tissues exceeding 60 parts per million.

Food chains as simple as the one in the model ecosystem make fine examples, but reality usually isn't that simple. Even an ecosystem of very limited dimensions will contain dozens, perhaps hundreds, of

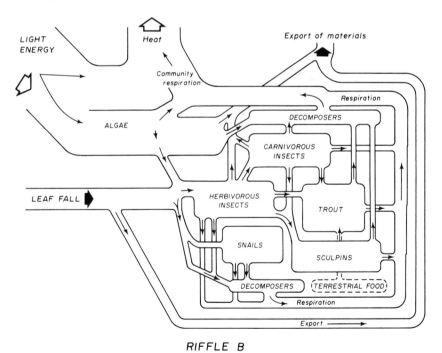

RIFFLE B

Figure 8.3. A food web for a riffle in Berry Creek, Oregon. "Export" refers to biomass leaving the system. (Courtesy of Dr. Charles E. Warren and W. B. Saunders Co.)

species. Some species may be dominant during one season, while others may be dominant all year. And keeping tabs on an ecosystem is difficult because some animals are omnivores, feeding both on producers and consumers, and some feed at different levels during different stages of their life cycles. So the term "food chain" may be a little misleading. "Food web" much more accurately describes the situation that exists in the typical, balanced ecosystem, with its many interdependent species (Figure 8.3). The addition or removal of a single species usually has far-reaching effects within the community, because the web must then undergo a restructuring process. Figure 8.3 shows the placement of trout in the food web of a specific ecosystem — but it isn't meant to show their exact location in *all* situations; food webs, like individuals, exhibit a high degree of variability.

When death comes to top level consumers, or to any individuals that weren't used as food, the decomposers break them down and their chemicals are liberated, perhaps soon again to become incorporated into living tissue. However, the solar energy initially stored in sugar molecules by producers has been dissipated and is no longer available for biological use. Life continues only because more solar energy is being photosynthetically fixed by new generations of producers.

Foods Consumed by Trout

Salmonids are carnivores, able to make use of a broad spectrum of animal life for food. In most ecosystems in which they live the greatest part of their diet consists of aquatic insects. But because food webs are highly individual, the foods consumed by trout in any given ecosystem depend upon what prey species are present as well as on their respective seasonal abundances. Diets also change as trout grow. It's well known, for example, that as browns become larger they tend to consume greater porportions of fish. And individuals within a given body of water may have strong preferences for certain food items.

Since no two ecosystems are precisely alike, one of the tasks that confronts an angler seeking intimate knowledge of a piece of trout water is to determine what food items are important in the diets of resident fish. Table 8.1 was compiled from several tables that appeared in 1940 in Paul Needham's book *Trout Streams* and is based on his analysis of the stomach contents of several hundred brook, brown and rainbow trout. Data from Needham's tables have been cited a number of times in various articles dealing with trout food, and even though the per-

Table 8.1. Food items found in stomachs of three species of trout

Food Item	Brook Trout (N = 251) 3–9 Inches Long		Brown Trout (N = 46) 5–12 Inches Long		Rainbow Trout (N = 80) 3–12 Inches Long	
	Number	% of Total	Number	% of Total	Number	% of Total
Caddiceflies	1,223	30.0	230	9.5	247	18.7
Two-winged flies	755	18.5	61	2.5	234	17.8
Mayflies	716	17.6	1,907	79.3	490	37.1
Beetles	268	6.6	28	1.2	105	7.9
Spring-tails	264	6.5	—	—	—	—
Leaf-hoppers	260	6.4	17	0.7	13	1.0
Ants, bees, wasps	123	3.0	22	1.0	88	6.6
Crayfish, scuds	69	1.7	15	0.7	13	1.0
Grasshoppers	66	1.6	7	0.3	7	0.5
Stoneflies	61	1.5	17	0.7	44	3.3
True bugs	48	1.2	—	—	11	0.8
Earthworms	47	1.1	51	2.1	—	—
Snails	35	0.8	—	—	14	1.1
Fish, salamanders	21	0.5	9	0.3	6	0.5
Slugs	—	—	30	1.3	—	—
Moth larvae	—	—	—	—	17	1.2
Alderfly larvae	—	—	—	—	11	0.8
Miscellaneous	122	3.0	10	0.4	23	1.7
Totals	4,078	100	2,404	100	1,323	100

SOURCE: Based on data from Paul Needham's 1940 book, *Trout Streams.*

centages shown can be considered typical, they shouldn't be thought of as dogma.

Survivorship

Life in ecosystems in which trout are found isn't easy. A multitude of environmental pressures such as competition, adverse temperature and chemical conditions, predation, and disease act in such a way that not all individuals in a population attain the life span of which they're potentially capable.

It's a principle of biology that the potential for increase in numbers of any species is greater than is necessary for the maintenance of a status quo population: under normal conditions, species produce excessive numbers of offspring. Naturally this means that some of them will have to go — to perish by the wayside. It has been an article of faith with biologists since Darwin that those offspring best capable of coping with the adversities doled out by a given ecosystem are going to be the survivors.

Starting out with a number of individuals beginning life at the same time (hatching, in the case of salmonids), and plotting the death rate as the group progresses through life, gives a survivorship curve like the one shown in Figure 8.4. The survivorship curve for a typical trout population reveals that mortality is extremely high during the fry stage, and that if trout can make it through this hazardous period their chances for continued survival improve greatly. Actually, survivorship curves for different trout populations vary from one another, but the fact remains that most trout die very young — long before they have a chance to spawn.

Age and Growth
The task of accumulating data in the field isn't easy. The mere determination of the age of fish can be a problem, and the sample used for data collection has to be large enough to reflect the true nature of the entire population. The instabilities of ecosystems have to be kept in mind, and the hosts of environmental factors that vary from year to year, either favoring or hindering optimal growth, successful reproduction, and survival, have to be accounted for. If a biologist takes a sample of trout today, he may come up with a different set of data than he would using a sample taken on the same date three or four years later. Studies that cover larger time spans generally provide a greater wealth of information about trout populations than studies of shorter duration do.

Sometimes hypothetical situations are best for showing what goes

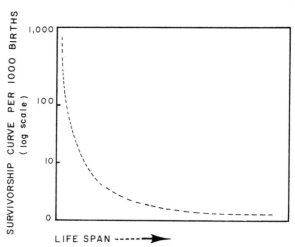

Figure 8.4. Survivorship curve for trout (see text for explanation). The curve is based on information from a variety of sources and may be considered "typical."

Table 8.2. Mean lengths and weights of trout of given ages in a hypothetical population

Year		Mean Length (in.)	Mean Weight (oz.)
0	(at hatching)	1.00	0.0035
0.5	(6 mos.)	1.75	0.038
1		3.00	0.18
2		7.00	2.3
3		10.00	6.9
4		12.00	11.8
5		13.75	17.8
6		15.25	24.3
7		16.50	30.7

on in a complex set of events, because with them you can idealize and simplify in order to keep things clear. Age and growth in trout populations is one of those areas that lends itself to this kind of approach. The hypothetical trout population dealt with in the following pages is based on published studies, and represents a typical life situation. In this population sac fry average one inch in length at hatching. And since only rare individuals survive beyond the age of seven, they aren't included.

Table 8.2 shows the average (mean) lengths and weights for trout at various ages. And with that information it's possible to construct graphs that clearly and simply show the relationships between age and length (Figure 8.5), age and weight (Figure 8.6) and length and weight

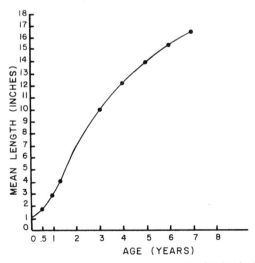

Figure 8.5. Growth curve showing average (mean) lengths of individuals in existing age groups in a hypothetical trout population.

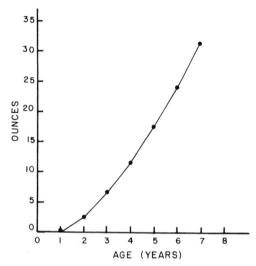

Figure 8.6. Growth curve showing average (mean) weights of individuals in existing age groups in a hypothetical trout population.

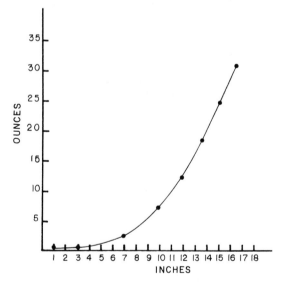

Figure 8.7. Curve expressing the relationship of length to weight in a hypothetical trout population.

(Figure 8.7). The slopes of such growth curves can vary considerably from one ecosystem to another, and a biologist studying a specific trout population would certainly want to know its growth characteristics. He'd probably want to study any changes in growth patterns over time within the population, perhaps to see what effects management practices may have had; and he might also wish to compare his trout population's curves with growth curves for populations of other areas.

One method of population study is to follow the progress of a number of individuals of similar age — a group called a cohort — from the beginning of life until death. A population in the wild isn't made up of a single cohort, but of many: each year class (the trout hatched in a particular year) represents a cohort. And because environmental conditions vary from year to year, so will mortalities. But by isolating a single, typical year class (cohort) for study, the impact that an ecosystem has on a total population can be more easily understood. The survivorship curve reflects just such an approach, and Table 8.3 is designed to show survivorship for a cohort of 100,000 newly hatched trout from the hypothetical population already examined. Length and weight information correspond to that already given in Table 8.2. Since it's now known how many trout have made it to a certain age, it's possible to estimate the total weight of the cohort at any given time (in other words, the standing crop).

Within a given cohort, 350 ounces of sac fry hatch. Early mortality is so high that at three months the surviving members, though they have grown substantially as individuals, together weight only 162

Table 8.3. Total biomass values for surviving members of a hypothetical cohort of trout at various times within a total lifespan

Age	Number in Population		Average (Mean) Weight per Individual (oz.)		Population weight (oz.)		Population weight (lbs.)
0 (at hatching)	100,000	×	0.0035	=	350	=	21.88
3 mos.	9,000	×	0.018	=	162	=	10.13
6 mos.	4,400	×	0.038	=	167.2	=	10.45
9 mos.	3,400	×	0.078	=	265.2	=	16.58
1 yr.	2,900	×	0.18	=	522	=	32.63
2 yrs.	950	×	2.3	=	2,185	=	136.56
3 yrs.	240	×	6.9	=	1,656	=	103.50
4 yrs.	68	×	11.8	=	802.4	=	50.15
5 yrs.	14	×	17.8	=	249.2	=	15.58
6 yrs.	5	×	24.3	=	121.5	=	7.59
7 yrs.	2	×	30.7	=	61.4	=	3.84

ounces. Thereafter, mortality decreases sufficiently and growth increases at such a pace that the maximum standing crop is attained at the age of two. From that point on, cohort weight decreases until, in the seventh year, there are a few good-sized fish of around two pounds.

Survival and Production

The figures in table 8.3 are for those trout that have survived to a certain time, but they include no information on trout which died between the times data was recorded. Nevertheless, consideration of these trout is relevant, because the ecosystem has provided for their creation. And an efficient use of the ecosystem is what trout management endeavors to accomplish. Table 8.4 gives values for the amounts (weights) of trout tissue that have been produced and have perished. The same thing is also shown graphically in Figure 8.8, which shows all of the trout tissue produced within the cohort and all that died, as well as the standing crop over time: it represents just about all we know concerning the cohort.[2]

In terms of efficiency, it might at first appear that the best use of the ecosystem could be made by harvesting trout of about one and a half years. At that time, the greatest percentage of trout flesh that has been produced is still alive. And small trout apply a greater proportion

Table 8.4. Biomass values, including cumulative data for a hypothetical cohort of trout

	Total Tissue Produced during Period (oz.)	Total Tissue Produced (Cumulative) (oz.)	Biomass Dying during Period (oz.)	Biomass Dying (Cumulative) (oz.)	Biomass Alive at End of Period (oz.)
0 at hatching)	350	350	—	—	350
0-3 mos.	546	896	734	734	162
3-6 mos.	72.2	968.2	67	801	167.2
6-9 mos.	166	1,134.2	68	869	265.2
9-12 mos.	373.8	1,508	117	986	522
1-2 yrs.	3,858	5,366	2,195	3,181	2,185
2-3 yrs.	2,357	7,723	2,886	6,067	1,656
3-4 yrs.	702.4	8,425.4	1,556	7,623	802.4
4-5 yrs.	152.8	8,578.2	706	8,329	249.2
5-6 yrs.	81.3	8,659.5	209	8,538	121.5
6-7 yrs.	37.9	8,697.4	98	8,636	61.4

NOTE: See text for discussion. The three boxed figures relate directly to Figure 8.8.

2. To show the relationship of the table and the graph, the boxed values in Table 8.4 are shown again in Figure 8.8.

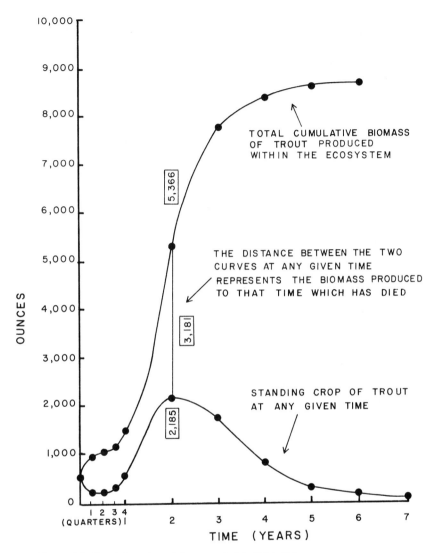

Figure 8.8. Graph based on data presented in Table 8.4.

of their food toward growth than big trout do, and they feed lower in the food chain.

But things other than efficiency have to be considered. Quite aside from the fact that a four-inch trout isn't a desirable item for anglers, there's the question of reproduction. The cohort represents only one year class of a population which presumably exists over a long period of time. If the cohort represents an average year class for the population, and if the population is self-sustaining, the egg production

Table 8.5. Egg production for trout of various ages in the hypothetical cohort

Age	Number of Trout[a]	Mean Number of Eggs per Female	Total Egg Production
2	950	200	95,000
3	240	480	57,600
4	68	730	24,820
5	14	1,000	7,000
6	5	1,300	3,250
7	2	1,800	1,800
			189,470

[a]Assuming an equal proportion of males and females

of the cohort should be sufficient to produce 100,000 sac fry, or approximately that number, since population fluctuations are to be expected. Assuming that these trout spawn by the age of two, we might expect them to produce (potentially) between 180,000 and 190,000 eggs. This estimate is based on the average egg yields that have been found for fish within the cohort (Table 8.5). The numbers and sizes of eggs produced by trout vary considerably, depending upon species and genetic strain, on water quality, and on nutrition during egg development. But the values given in Table 8.5 are realistic.

With what has been learned about the hypothetical trout population from studying the cohort — a typical year class — it might seem wise to set a size limit of eight or nine inches on trout caught by anglers. Such a limit would allow fish to spawn once before facing the prospect of the creel. Where angling pressure is low, a lower size limit would be acceptable or even desirable. Setting a size limit too high doesn't permit the efficient use of the ecosystem because it allows more of the trout produced to succumb to natural causes. If, for example, a size limit of 12 inches (the mean length at age four in the cohort) was set, a tremendous amount of trout flesh would perish before anglers could even begin to realize a harvest.[3] There's also the strong probability that removing some members of the population early in life allows the survivors a larger share of the available food and a broader selection of the available feeding stations and cover areas. By extension, these conditions should favor increased growth and improve chances for further survival.

3. The amount of trout flesh that would die by age four can be seen graphically by noting the distance between the two curves in Figure 8.8 at four years.

Management of Trout Populations

Many anglers associate trout with wilderness settings and find the very idea of managed populations a bit offensive. But management doesn't have to mean activity as radical and conspicuous as put-and-take fishing. Even states possessing true wilderness trout populations have statewide size and catch limits, so by definition their wilderness trout are being managed to a degree. And when considering the growing armies of anglers searching for quality trout fishing, even wilderness purists have to concede that there's plenty of need for good management.

Limits on Size and Number
The fundamental aim of setting size and catch limits is to manage a trout population in order to get a maximum harvest of fish, while allowing for the survival (maintenance) of trout stocks. By and large, the changes that take place over time in the biomass of an exploited trout population depend upon what is known as recruitment — fish joining the exploitable population when they reach the legal size — and upon growth, death from natural causes and being caught.

Population biomass at end of time period	=	Population biomass at beginning of time period	+	Biomass gained by RECRUITMENT and GROWTH	−	Biomass lost through NATURAL DEATH and HARVEST

If, over time, recruitment and growth of trout equals natural death and harvest, the total amount of trout tissue in the exploitable population will remain unchanged, even though there has been some turnover. In such a case, the trout population is said to be in equilibrium. But a totally unfished population may also be in equilibrium: there would simply be no harvest; all deaths would result from natural causes. Similarly, if an unreasonably high size limit was placed on the population, a very few large fish would be caught, and, equilibrium could be established in time. In both cases the population, though in equilibrium, would be underfished from the standpoint of obtaining a maximum harvest of fish.

A grossly overfished population of trout may be in equilibrium if, for example, a bare minimum number of spawners are allowed to survive to maintain a skeleton population. In this case the harvest, though primarily responsible for keeping the population at a low level, would also be small, and anglers would have to spend many man-hours fishing in order to take a trout. The point is that between the extremes of underfishing and overfishing there's a level of harvest that permits a maximum yield from a population on a sustained basis (Figure 8.9).

By setting size and catch limits, the part of a population that can be fished and the numbers of trout that can be harvested from that part can be defined. Many considerations can be involved in defining those limits. Take the case of Wisconsin's Lawrence Creek (Adams County), a brook trout stream where considerable research has been done. On the basis of fishing demand on the creek, it was determined that a sizable number of yearling trout (pre-spawners) were needed within the exploitable population in order to reduce the fishing pressure on older trout (brood fish). A six-inch limit had essentially the same effect as no limit at all, because by midsummer nearly all the yearlings had attained that size, but a nine-inch limit was too high, since so few yearlings reached nine inches that virtually the only legal trout were the older brood fish that needed protection. The upshot was that experimental size limits of seven and eight inches were set.

Fishing can also be controlled by limiting angling to certain defined seasons, and by banning fishing in areas where a population is exceptionally vulnerable to exploitation, such as on spawning grounds. And, the means of harvest can be controlled: more and more, areas are being closed to all but fly fishing — and because trout are above all

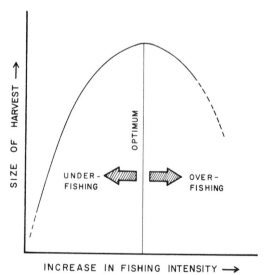

Figure 8.9. Graph showing the size of harvest (in terms of biomass) in relation to fishing intensity. The curve is for an equilibrium population and indicates the fishing intensity that will allow an optimum yield on a sustained basis.

creatures associated with refined sport, such measures usually don't meet with many objections.

The Management and Improvement of Habitat

Sometimes steps are taken to provide better conditions for the reproduction, growth and survival of salmonids, and to protect them from the destructive forces that seem to threaten constantly from all directions. Pollution, construction activity, and damage by livestock all take their toll on habitat. And so does stream channelization, that most destructive and damnable of practices, long defended by the Soil Conservation Service just because ditches can move water with greater speed and efficiency than most natural watercourses.

Habitat improvement consists primarily of the use of natural objects and phenomena (rocks, vegetation, sunlight, and the like) to maximum advantage to make a habitat more favorable for the desired species. Some improvement amounts to restoration of a destroyed habitat. Because our frontier ethic involved the view that nature's bounty was virtually limitless, a lot of good trout water has been abused.

It's important that water in trout streams be kept moving freely. Where dams are built, ponds are created in which suspended materials settle to the bottom, and which warm up with prolonged exposure to sunlight. Because silt bottoms and high water temperatures are unfavorable conditions for trout, larger dams are generally done away with when trout habitats are restored.

Natural watercourses are inclined to meander, and where gradients are steep enough they have a tendency to develop a "stairway" of alternating pools and riffles. Both situations can provide some excellent trout habitat. In addition to giving greater total length to a stream, meanders offer depth and protection on the outside of their bends; and pools offer the protection of depth, while riffles produce food and serve as spawning areas. Both meanders and pool-riffle arrangements can be enhanced by the proper placement of in-stream devices.

Before World War II, much of the habitat modification that was carried out did little to improve conditions for trout, even though done with the best of intentions. But the experience gained in those days has made recent approaches more successful, and devices have been designed that enable biologists to use the power of flowing water to create better trout habitat. Stone and log deflectors are used to speed up current where it has slowed so much that siltation is a threat. In high gradient streams, very low dams (perhaps a foot or two in height) can be built if upstream riffles won't be inundated and if the current is strong enough to prevent the settling of sediments; the plunge pools that result offer fine protection for trout. Cover can be created in some spots by building overhangs from a bank, and submerged brush provides an abundance of feeding stations if properly located. Banks especially vulnerable to erosion at high water stages may be protected by rock revetments, which can supply additional trout cover. And if water temperatures tend to be uncomfortably high for trout, the effluent from nearby springs can sometimes be diverted directly into the stream.

The types and amounts of vegetation along a trout stream play a dominant role in the formation of quality habitat. Heavily forested banks often lead to low trout production, since shade from the forest canopy impedes photosynthesis and, therefore, the growth of aquatic producers. The effect of overshading may be seen not only within the food chain, but also in the absence of some aquatic plant forms that offer cover for fish. Streamside trees are therefore sometimes removed to admit light.

One of the most suitable types of vegetation for the banks of trout streams consists of grasses and low bushes that hang down into the water to provide trout cover. The dense root systems also hold up bank soil, and with stable banks the current tends to dig a deeper channel rather than a wider one — a condition also favorable to trout. Vegetation of this kind is easily damaged by livestock, so protective fences are frequently placed along trout streams that meander through farm country.

Fertilization is sometimes suggested to increase the growth of aquatic plants, but this calls for a delicate approach, because excessive fertilizer could lead to eutrophication. In areas where there's already considerable agricultural runoff, increased fertility is about the last thing needed.

There have been reports of supplemental feeding experiments in which fish foods were introduced directly into trout waters. Even though the results — in terms of fish poundage yielded — have sometimes been good, this approach is much narrower than one which deals with the ecosystem as a whole; and it takes trout a big step closer to the realm of domestic beasts dependent on people for handouts.

Habitat for spawning is managed by protecting riffles and by removing silt-depositing dams. Since spawning areas are frequently shallow and unprotected, trout are especially vulnerable while breeding, so cover is often made available nearby. In some waters in which suitable gravel is lacking artificial spawning beds have been constructed with some success, but the techniques are expensive and not widely applied at present.

Fewer habitat improvement measures can be taken in lakes because of their sheer volume. Fertilization is occasionally attempted and various means are used (compressed air, for example) to raise dissolved oxygen levels if winterkill or summerkill threatens. Stream improvement methods can be applied to inlets and outlets. Habitats in larger streams require less work, as a rule, than those in streams of modest proportions. Bigger waters usually provide plenty of depth for cover, and they're wide enough to keep trees along the banks from blocking out the necessary sunlight. Many streams offer unique wilderness settings that shouldn't be tampered with; in such streams, management becomes largely a matter of preservation.

Trout fishermen instinctively appreciate wilderness aesthetics. For biologists, such aesthetics can be a problem, because it is often difficult to blend their handiwork in with the wrack and randomness of a natural situation. It's well understood, though, that trout aren't best pursued in a synthetic environment cluttered with engineering marvels, and when trout habitat is being managed or improved, aesthetics are usually given high priority.

Artificial Propagation

Angling pressure is so intense in some areas that overfishing of trout stocks is unavoidable. One of the most fruitful solutions to this problem has been the establishment of trout hatcheries, which might be thought of as artificial and highly simplified ecosystems designed to maximize the production of trout flesh and to minimize trout mortality.

Hatchery fish may be introduced in a single operation into water initially lacking in trout. Quite a few alpine lakes in the Rockies offer outstanding wilderness fishing because of such seedings. Stocking can also be done on a periodic basis in waters offering a suitable habitat, but incapable of sustaining significant spawning populations. And trout can be stocked where reproducing populations already exist just to increase their numbers and to provide some measure of angling success to hordes of fishermen.

Many biologists are opposed to stocking legal-sized trout if naturally reproducing populations are already present in a given water, because stocking results in a sudden rise in competition for the available food and space, to the detriment of native and hatchery fish alike. When large brown trout of hatchery origin are released, the native trout sometimes decrease numerically, perhaps as a result of cannibalism. And the introduction of fish into waters containing unique genetic strains of native trout, which are especially adapted to local conditions, can be a serious and irrevocable mistake. Stocking is now viewed as something a bit less than the panacea it was once considered to be. It's just another tool that the fisheries biologist can use after making an adequate survey — and then it should be used with care.

Managing Other Species

Wild salmonids are always part of a complex web of interdependent species, so their success within an ecosystem hinges directly or indirectly on the legions of other creatures also found in the community. Sometimes it may be advisable to introduce food organisms for the benefit of trout. And if one species or another appears to be especially detrimental to resident trout populations, measures can be taken to reduce its numbers.

Competition from other species most often takes the form of predation and of overlapping food or space requirements. But some creatures, such as rough fish that stir up bottom sediments, may render the available habitat less fit for trout. Other species may transmit parasites to trout, and although disease and parasite control is not usually attempted on wild fish, some parasitic diseases can be combatted by reducing the numbers of non-salmonid organisms that serve as hosts in the parasite life cycles.

If the control or removal of a species is required, the task can be approached by doing away with restrictions on its harvest, by netting, by shocking with various electronic devices or by using selective poisons. The sea lampreys that were unintentionally introduced into the Great Lakes, and which created so much havoc among the lake trout populations, provide a classic example. A number of methods have been used against the lampreys, including electric weirs and poisons that act selectively against their larval stage.

In some instances, it's most appropriate simply to remove all fish from a body of water. This is done by using a degradable poison that acts against all fish species. After the fish have perished and the poison has degraded into harmless breakdown products, biologists can begin anew by stocking just those species desired.

Yet it isn't always a good idea to do away with what appear to be objectionable species. Because ecosystems are so complex, changing the relative abundances of species may yield undesirable results.

Eliminating predators, for instance, may indeed cause trout populations to rise, but the crowding that results can lead to stunted fish. Interference with the species composition of an ecosystem requires a broad approach, and the kind of expertise and experience that allows the final result to be envisioned.

If trout are really just small cogs in the machinery of their ecosystems, it's clear that the frequent references to trout water in angling literature reflect a preoccupation with these fish. We maintain and improve ecosystems so they'll be most favorable for trout, and by regulating our harvests we seek to get the most (and the best) trout that an ecosystem can provide on a sustained basis — all the while trying to retain the aesthetic qualities peculiar to the ecosystems containing trout. It's said that nothing in nature is unrelated; and since this is so, there's a lot to be gained by seeing these fish not merely as isolated entities, but as parts of a large picture of great complexity and intelligible pattern.

Selected Readings
Index

Selected Readings

CHAPTER 1: EVOLUTION IN SALMONIDAE

Behnke, R. J. 1972. The systematics of salmonid fishes of recently glaciated lakes. *Journal of the Fisheries Research Board of Canada* 29: 639-671.
This paper should be read by anyone interested in the evolution of salmonids.

Kosswig, C. 1963. Ways of speciation in fishes. *Copeia* (1963): 238-244.

Legendre, P., Schreck, C. B. and Behnke, R. J. 1972. Taximetric analysis of selected groups of western North American *Salmo* with respect to phylogenetic divergences. *Systematic Zoology* 28: 292-307.
This paper covers some of the more modern techniques being used to solve problems in salmonid classification, and applies them directly to many of the species, subspecies, "races," etc. of trout found in the western part of the continent.

Mayr, E. 1970. *Populations, species and evolution: an abridgement of animal species and evolution.* Cambridge, Mass.: Belknap Press of Harvard University Press.
A short version of a standard text on evolution. It deals with major principles.

Rounsefell, G. A. 1962. *Relationships among North American Salmonidae.* Washington, D.C.: U.S. Fish and Wildlife Fishery Bulletin No. 209, pp. 235-269.

Vladykov, V. D. 1963. A review of salmonid genera and their broad geographical distribution. *Transactions of the Royal Society of Canada,* ser. 4, vol. 1, sec. 3: 459-504.

CHAPTER 2: INHERITANCE IN TROUT

Buss, K. W., and Wright, J. E. 1956. Results of species hybridization within the family salmonidae. *Progressive Fish Culturist* 18, pt. 4: 149-158.
This paper gives the results of a host of crosses between various species of salmonids.

Buss, K. W., and Wright, J. E. 1958. Appearance and fertility of trout hybrids. *Transactions of the American Fisheries Society* 87: 541-551.
This paper was published for the expressed purpose of presenting photographs of various hybrids. Typical specimens of both sexes are included.

Hines, N. O. 1976. *Fish of rare breeding: salmon and trout of the Donaldson strains.* Washington, D.C.: Smithsonian Institution Press.
The book gives an account of a long-term breeding program centered in the Pacific Northwest.

Chapter 3: The Salmonid Body

Gosline, W. A. 1970. *Functional morphology and classification of teleostean fishes.* Honolulu: University of Hawaii Press.
A general reference work on the anatomy of bony fishes.

Greene, C. W. and Greene, C. H. 1913. The skeletal musculature of the king salmon.
U.S. Bureau of Fisheries *Bulletin* 33: 25-59.
A thorough and technical treatment of muscles in salmonids. Includes details of muscles in head and fins. A classic paper that is well illustrated.

Henderson, N. E. 1967. The urinary and genital systems of trout. *Journal of the Fisheries Research Board of Canada* 24: 447-449.

Hoar, W. S., and Randall, D. J. 1969-1971. *Fish Physiology.* 5 vol. New York: Academic Press.
This major reference work would be useful to anyone with a specific question about the physiology of trout.

Love, R. M. 1970. *The chemical biology of fishes.* New York: Academic Press.
A general reference on physiology.

Parker, T. J., and Haswell, W. A. 1963. *A Textbook of Zoology.* 7th ed. New York: Macmillan Co.
Although a general zoology text, its authors use the brown trout as a model animal. Coverage is very good.

Satchell, G. H. 1971. *Circulation in fishes.* Cambridge, England: University of Cambridge Press.

Smith, L. S. and Bell, G. R. 1975. *A practical guide to the anatomy and physiology of pacific salmon.* Miscellaneous special publication 27, Department of the Environment, Fisheries and Marine Service, Ottawa, Canada.
This is a concise and beautifully illustrated work that would be a worthy addition to any trout angler's bookshelf. Obtainable through Information Canada, Ottawa K1A 0S9, Canada.

Young, J. Z. 1962. *The life of vertebrates.* 2nd ed. New York: Oxford University Press.
A comprehensive reference work on vertebrates.

Chapter 4: The Larger Parasites of Salmonids

Amlacher, E. 1961. *Textbook of fish diseases.* 1970 translation by D. A. Conroy and R. L. Herman. Neptune, N.J.: T. F. H. Publications.

Hoffman, G. L. 1967. *Parasites of North American freshwater fishes,* Neptune, N.J.: T. F. H. Publications.
Lavishly illustrated with color photographs of parasites and infected hosts.

U.S. Department of the Interior. 1971. *List of reference sources for students of fish diseases.* Leaflet FDL-33, U.S. Department of the Interior, Bureau of Sport Fisheries and Wildlife, Division of Fishery Research. Washington, D.C.
Gives sources of information on specific diseases and parasites.

CHAPTER 5: THE AQUATIC MEDIUM

Coker, R. E. 1964. *Streams, lakes, ponds.* Chapel Hill, North Carolina: University of North Carolina Press.
A general reference work.

Frey, D. G., ed. 1963. *Limnology in North America.* Madison: University of Wisconsin Press.
A general reference for the study of fresh waters.

Hynes, H. B. N. 1970. *The ecology of running waters.* Liverpool, England: Liverpool University Press.
An excellent reference work.

Leopold, L. B., Wolman, M. G., and Miller, J. P. 1964. *Fluvial processes in geomorphology.* San Francisco: W. H. Freeman and Co.
Deals primarily with the role of streams in sculpting the landscape.

Morisawa, M. 1968. *Streams: their dynamics and morphology.* New York: McGraw-Hill Book Co.
Though short, this is a good reference work on streams.

Reid, G. K. 1961. *Ecology of inland waters and estuaries.* New York: Reinhold Publishing Corp.
A general reference book.

Ruttner, F. 1964. *Fundamentals of limnology.* 3d ed. Toronto: University of Toronto Press.
An excellent general text on fresh waters.

Warren, C. E. 1971. *Biology and water pollution control.* Philadelphia: W. B. Saunders.
Although the title suggests a narrow approach, this is comprehensive and superbly written. The section on natural waters is excellent, as is the entire book.

CHAPTER 6: NONREPRODUCTIVE BEHAVIOR

Adron, J. W., Grant, P. T., and Cowey, C. B. 1973. A system for the quantitative study of the learning capacity of rainbow trout and its application to the study of food preferences and behaviour. *Journal of Fish Biology* 5: 625-636.

Bryan, J. E. 1973. Feeding history, parental stock, and food selection in rainbow trout. *Behaviour* 45: 123-153.

Bryan, J. E., and Larkin, P. A. 1972. Food specialization by individual trout. *Journal of the Fisheries Research Board of Canada* 29: 1615-1624.

Ginetz, R. M., and Larkin, P. A. 1973. Choice of colors and food items by rainbow trout *(Salmo gairdneri). Journal of the Fisheries Research Board of Canada* 30: 229-234.

Jenkins, T. M. 1969. *Social structure, position choice and microdistribution of two trout species (Salmo trutta and Salmo gairdneri) resident in mountain streams.* Animal Behaviour. Monographs vol. 2. London: Bailliere, Tindall and Cassell, pp. 57-123.
Should be read by anyone interested in trout behavior.

Kwain, Wen-Hwa, and MacCrimmon, H. 1967. The behavior and bottom color selection of the rainbow trout, *Salmo gairdneri* Richardson, exposed to different light intensities. *Animal Behaviour* 15: 75-78.

CHAPTER 7: REPRODUCTIVE BEHAVIOR

Banks, J. W. 1969. A review of the literature on the upstream migration of adult salmonids. *Journal of Fish Biology* 1: 85-136.

Fabricius, E., and Gustafson, K. J. 1954. *Further aquarium observations on the spawning behaviour of the char, Salvelinus alpinus L.* Institute of Freshwater Research, Drottningholm, no. 35, pp. 58-104.

Jones, J. W., and Ball, J. N. 1954. The spawning behaviour of brown trout and salmon. *British Journal of Animal Behaviour* 2: 103-114.
    A classic study, perhaps the *classic study, of salmonid spawning behavior.*

Royce, W. F. 1951. *Breeding habits of lake trout in New York.* Washington, D.C.: U.S. Fish and Wildlife Service Fishery Bulletin no. 59, pp. 59-76.

CHAPTER 8: TROUT POPULATIONS AND TROUT PRODUCTION

Allen, K. R. 1951. *The Horokiwi stream: a study of a trout population.* Fisheries Bulletin no. 10, Wellington, New Zealand: New Zealand Marine Department.
    An all-time classic study of a trout population.

Allen, K. R. 1952. *A New Zealand trout stream: some facts and figures.* Fisheries Bulletin no. 10A, Wellington, New Zealand: New Zealand Marine Department.
    A shorter and more readable version of Allen's 1951 publication.

Carlander, K. D. 1969. *Handbook of freshwater fishery biology.* Iowa City: University of Iowa Press.
    One of the reference works most often consulted by fisheries biologists. Full of information on salmonids.

McFadden, J. T. 1961. *A population study of brook trout, Salvelinus fontinalis.* Wildlife Monographs no. 7, November 1961, Washington, D.C.: Wildlife Society.
    A classic study.

Needham, P. R. 1940. *Trout streams.* Ithaca, N.Y.: Comstock Publishing Co.
    An old book, but it still contains relevant information and is found on many angler's bookshelves.

Russell-Hunter, W. D. 1970. *Aquatic productivity.* New York: Macmillan Co.
    A general reference work.

Warren, C. E. 1971. *Biology and water pollution control.* Philadelphia: W. B. Saunders.

Weatherly, A. H. 1972. *Growth and ecology of fish populations.* New York: Academic Press.
    A general reference book.

White, R. J., and Brynildson, O. M. 1967. *Guidelines for management of trout stream habitat in Wisconsin.* Technical Bulletin no. 39, Wisconsin Department of Natural Resources, Madison.
    This abundantly illustrated work covers a variety of approaches to habitat improvement.

Index

DESIGNED BY QUENTIN FIORE
COMPOSED BY TOTAL TYPE, MADISON, WISCONSIN
MANUFACTURED BY FAIRFIELD GRAPHICS, FAIRFIELD, PENNSYLVANIA
TEXT AND DISPLAY LINES ARE SET IN GARTH GRAPHIC

Library of Congress Cataloging in Publication Data
Willers, W. B., 1938–
Trout biology, an angler's guide.
Bibliography: pp. 195–198
Includes index.
1. Trout.   2. Trout fishing.   I. Title.
QL638.S2W55   597′.55   81-50829
ISBN 0-299-08720-4   AACR2